THE WORKING MAN & WOMAN'S GUIDE TO BECOMING A

# MILLIONAIRE

## AL HERRON

*with* SALLIE B. MIDDLEBROOK, PH.D.

Printed in the United States of America by
Taylor Publishing
1550 West Mockingbird Lane
Dallas, TX 75235

**Discount book purchases:**
Books written by Al Herron are available at quantity
discounts with bulk purchase for educational, business or
sales promotional use. For information, please write to:

Prentiss Publishing Company, LLC
5801 Marvin D. Love Frwy., Ste. 103
Dallas, TX 75237

or

P.O. Box 764265
Dallas, TX 75376-4265

Official Prentiss Publishing Web Site:
www.prentisspublishing.com

ISBN 0-9778607-0-1

*Cover photo:*     Montaque, Studio Milano Photography
*Cover design:*    Sallie B. Middlebrook
*Page design:*     Florence McLure

# Dedication

This book is warmly and sincerely dedicated to:
My wife, Lela Herron
My mother, Ella Herron
My father, Matthew Herron
My friend, mentor, and business partner, C. A. Galloway

My work ethic comes from my mother and father. My mother had the ability to take a small amount of anything and make it stretch to serve a lot of people. She knew how to save money when she only had a little to start with. She passed these lessons on to me by example, and for that, I am truly grateful.

My father was the first entrepreneur in our family. With very little education, he was able to acquire land in Mississippi to operate a farm, and he also owned and ran a grocery store in our community. He laid the foundation—again mostly by example, that has helped me form the basis of my financial thinking. Because of this, I am truly blessed.

My business partner, C. A. Galloway, was the first black person to serve on the City Council of Dallas, and he founded Century 21 Galloway-Herron. A man of integrity, he made it possible for me not to have to start at the bottom. Mr. Galloway had no children to continue his name, but he wanted his business to continue into perpetuity. Because of his guidance and generosity, our business lives on with his name leading the way for the Galloway-Herron brand. For this, I am truly grateful to Mr. and Mrs. C. A. Galloway.

My wife, Lela, has been supportive and the love of my life for 34 years. Our children are Algernon, an outstanding son, and Latosha, a beautiful and fantastic daughter. Thank you all for all you do. Lela seems to know what I need even before I ask—and sometimes even before I know. What a blessing my family is to me, and I thank God for giving me the wisdom to see my blessings.

# Acknowledgments

I want to recognize and thank my staff at our Century 21 Galloway-Herron office. They are greatest people in the world to work with. Our top-notch agents have afforded me the freedom and peace of mind I had to have in order to spend quality time working on this book.

To my assistant, Johnnie Smith; to my daughter, Latosha Herron; to my son, Algernon; to my niece, Linda O'Neal, and to Evelyn Mays, Deborah Carter and Sherri Lampkin, you are all valued and vital members of my staff. You work so well together that our office runs like a well-oiled machine, with or without me. Thank you very much.

I would also like to thank and acknowledge the contributions of my co-author, Dr. Sallie B. Middlebrook. A native of Silver Creek, Mississippi (a town that's a stone's throw away from my hometown, Prentiss, Mississippi), she has played a key role in helping me to bring this project to the finish line. She has a background that includes many years teaching in higher education, plus working in areas of journalism and marketing, the subject area of her Ph.D. In fact, in addition to her work as a marketing and publishing consultant, she teaches part-time in the MBA program at a university in Houston. Sallie has truly utilized all her skills to help me put all the pieces of this book together. Without her, there is a good chance this book might still be on the drawing board.

# Contents

# Foreword

This book is a wonderful example of the power of giving through sharing what you know. Told from the down-to-earth perspective of a man who has not forgotten where he came from, within the pages of this book is a plan with great potential to help millions of everyday working people—like you and me—achieve extraordinary wealth. Primarily, it offers a strategy for developing a "millionaire mindset."

As of 2001, there were more than 5 million households in the United States with a net worth in excess of $1 million. More than 2.7 million of these households reported having at least $1 million in liquid assets—cash, and this wealth did not even include their homes. In the midst of all this affluence, still, the net worth of the average American household is now in the vicinity of about $45,000 (and it's a lot less for members of some minority groups). What's up with that? What is it that the millionaires know that the average working person does not?

This book will answer that question for you, and many more. I know this, because I know Al Herron. He is someone who has learned and used the principles and activities he speaks of in this book, and he communicates these ideas easily with people from all kinds of backgrounds. Therefore, although he is now a multimillionaire, he has not forgotten where he came from. Al Herron was not born into money, and he did not inherit millions. Like you and me, he always knew he had to work to earn money, but unlike most people, he learned early in life how to also make his money work for him.

Al is now sharing with you his formula for financial success. His plan is not magic, and it won't work unless you are ready to do what it teaches you how to do. But it represents a realistic light of hope for people who want to make the most of the money they work for every day. Using the plan set forth in this book, it is not only possible, it is inevitable that—if used as recommended, it will result in making an ordinary work-every-day-person, a millionaire.

This plan is not like those real-estate buying courses you see advertised on television where you have to buy countless items before you can get started. Instead, it is a simple plan that will teach you how to use your job as your opportunity to make your money work for you. If you have a job, or any type of sustaining income stream, you can implement this plan.

It all begins at the most essential part of the American Dream—home ownership—because it is an indispensable part of the millionaire mindset. Home ownership is also part of the course for learning to manage your financial life so that you can make your money do more for you. Al Herron is committed to helping millions who never dreamed of home ownership, to imagine it, and to realize this dream because he sees it as a critical part of becoming a millionaire.

In fact, I believe Al's plan can help achieve the home-ownership goal of the world's largest mortgage lender, Fannie Mae, in what it calls its "expanded" American Dream Commitment® (from the 2003 Fannie Mae National Housing Survey), which is to "create six million new homeowners (including 1.8 million minority families), over the next 10 years." This commitment aims to help families keep their homes, and to expand the supply of affordable homes where they are needed most. This book is going to do a lot to help achieve this goal because—step by step—it is going to walk millions of people who never thought they could buy a home through the home buying process on their way to becoming a millionaire.

Get ready to be informed, enlightened, entertained, and inspired. In this book, Al Herron uses his knowledge of the real estate business as well as his flair for story-telling, complete with examples from his own life and experiences to educate people about finance and money in a way that makes this plan easy to learn, and even easier to put into practice.

If you *are not* already a homeowner, this book will help speed you along the path to home ownership, an essential part of this plan to help make you a millionaire. If you *are* already a homeowner, this book will help you learn and apply more wisdom to the management of your savings and finances, so that you can take the steps you need to take to become a millionaire.

This book explains how you can execute Al's plan as quickly as you want, depending on how well and how swiftly you will put into action what he is teaching. Therefore, this book is a realistic and practical, back-to-basics kind of "textbook" teaching that no matter who you are or where you come from, you too can become a millionaire.

Al Herron is from rural Mississippi, and so am I. Just about everyone who knows anything (or who thinks anything) about rural Mississippi and about the rural south, sees it as a place populated by some of the nation's most financially downtrodden and economically challenged people. The part of rural Mississippi we're from 35 years ago was some of the most remote real estate in the state. It is an area about 70 miles south of Jackson, the state's capital city. Actually, I grew up in Silver Creek, Mississippi, which is located directly adjacent to Prentiss, Mississippi, Al's hometown. My father and mother both knew Al (and his parents and siblings) when he was a young teenager. In fact, my dad's baseball team played against Al and his younger team. And, when my brothers were very young, they got their hair cut in a barbershop where the building was owned by Al's dad.

I knew *of* him long before I met him, because—unbeknownst to him—he had become somewhat of a living legend among many who lived in the rural fringes of Lawrence and Jefferson Davis counties, where I grew up. His success became the topic of conversation among many parents and children living in our community because he had lifted himself up from his rural Mississippi upbringing. He had taken what God gave to him, what his parents instilled within him, and what the school system and the military taught him, to do more with his life. By telling their children about what Al was doing with his life, parents in my community were saying to their children "You too can do something great with your life."

No matter how far Al has progressed, he still keeps his humility and kindness intact. In 1987 and 1988, I worked for a small Dallas advertising and marketing agency owned by Joe Walker, one of Al's best friends. It was Joe who actually first introduced me to Al Herron, and now, I have had the opportunity to work with him in revising and expanding this wonderful book.

Al speaks to working people from all kinds of backgrounds using language and illustrations anyone can identify with. He talks about real people who have *real, everyday* problems such as those you and I face. He lays out an easy-to-understand and easy-to-follow plan for overcoming what might seem to be mountains too high to climb, on the path to financial freedom.

I think you're going to want to keep this book around for a long time, and even share it with your children, or other young people in your life. Because I know it will help them begin their financial life with a strong foundation of understanding about how to use a job to become a millionaire.

It has been a great honor, and a great learning experience, for me to help Al Herron with the writing, researching, publishing and marketing of this book. And even though, at this time, I am not a millionaire, like you, I want to use my faith and my God-given strengths and talents in a way that will allow me to manage and multiply my finances to the best of my ability. Therefore, I plan to implement all the principles and plans presented in this book because they represent sound advice that can only serve to benefit anyone who puts them into practice. But, like any good strategy for overcoming any human weakness, this plan will only work if you and I adhere to it.

By reading this book, I believe you'll gain much more than useful advice about how to attain financial success. Yes, you will become motivated to look for ways to improve your financial picture based on Al Herron's professional knowledge of finance and economics. And yes, you can follow this plan all the way to becoming a millionaire, just as Al did. Most of all, I think you'll be inspired by the sharing of his unwavering faith in God, the spiritual foundation allowing him to put into practice—every day of his life—principles that will undoubtedly help you improve your life in ways that go above and beyond financial prosperity.

Someone I know offers this excellent description and rationale for the power of giving through sharing. He says, think of yourself as being in a dark room with 100 people, and each person holds one candle. There are 101 unlit candles in this room, and you're holding the only match. With that match, you have the power to bring yourself and these other people out of the dark. Should you attempt to go around the room lighting candles using the one match? No, because your movement could cause that one light to go out. Therefore, the first thing you should do is to use the match to light your own candle. Next, you should use your candle to light one other person's candle. Then, the person whose candle you lit should use the light from his or her candle to light the next candle. This should continue until everyone's candle is lit. By working together, soon you're all in a room full of light, with 101 candles burning bright. There you are, surrounded by evidence that one light that is shared multiplies illumination, and lights a lot of paths.

That's exactly what this book is doing—sharing the light, and multiplying the illumination. I hope you will read it, internalize what it teaches, and begin implementing the plan Al recommends. I also hope you will share what you learn with someone else so that the lessons contained in *The Working Man and Woman's Guide to Becoming a Millionaire* can help illuminate a path to financial freedom for millions of people. Most of all, I hope this book will motivate you to want to live up to your best potential, inspiring you to seek and to discover a better life for yourself—in a brighter place with more light, and greater possibilities.

Sallie Beatrice Middlebrook, Ph.D.

Communications Consultant, Houston, Texas

Author of *Pray Every Day, A Single Woman's Prayer Guide For Hope and Victory Over Life's Recurring Themes*. (Available in Barnes and Noble and Borders bookstores nationwide, and on Amazon.com, BarnesandNoble.com; published by PublishAmerica, Baltimore, Maryland, 2005)

# Introduction

**Decide Where You're Going.**

At some point in your life, you have to decide where it is you want to go. Then, you must take off in that direction. If you have decided that where you are going in life involves becoming a millionaire, then this is the book that can help you get there.

Why can I say this with so much confidence? I can say it because I am someone who has worked all my life for a living, and I have used my job to launch my wealth-building campaign. And although it is good to be a millionaire, and to know you have all the money you will most likely need to live on, it is not always easy to admit you have arrived at this place of comfort and well being. Especially when you are someone from very humble beginnings as I am. But I had to tell you that I am a millionaire so that you will trust that I know how to make money. Now that you know I know how to make millions of dollars, I can teach you how to do the same thing.

And that is where my teaching begins—with acknowledging to you that I have arrived at that fantastical place in finance where so many millions of people are raring to go. How did I arrive here? I'll reveal the answer to this question throughout the steps of this book.

You know, a wise person once said when you see people having things that you want, but do not have, you can believe that these people know something that you do not know. So there is a good chance that the reason I have arrived here, and you have not, is because I know something that you do not.

Let us look now at what you <u>do</u> know. If you picked up this book because it says it is written for working men and women, that tells me you know at least one valuable thing. You know you need to work to make money. And that's good. Another thing it tells me is that you know you need to get and keep a job. However, knowing you need to work, and knowing you need to get and keep a job, obviously, is not enough. Why? Because even though you know how to get and keep a job, you—most likely, are still *not* a millionaire.

For the sake of teaching and learning, let us now go back over the stuff we know you know, right now.

1. You know you need to work to have an income.

2. You know you need to get and keep a job.

Good. So far, this learning process is pretty easy, isn't it? Now, let us look at what you <u>don't know</u> yet (And we're basing this conclusion solely on the fact that you are not now a millionaire). What you don't know includes the following:

How can you use *knowing* that you need to work to make money, along with *knowing* you need to get and keep a job, to make you a millionaire? That is the question. And this book is the answer. People all over America get and keep jobs all the time, but a job is usually not what will make you a millionaire.

The answer to my last question involves knowing how to make money *make* money, and that is why I have obtained financial success. And now that you have made the decision to become a millionaire, I can help you learn how to mak*e your* money *make* money.

By the way, I still go to work every day too, just like you. Why? Because I am not now, nor have I ever been a member of the "idle rich" crowd. I earned my money the old-fashioned way—I worked for it. Now, in addition to going to work every day, I am using what I know about making money to teach other people how to make it. Why am I doing this? Because the more I help other people, the more money I make. God has designed it that way. Helping others is one of the least known secrets to helping yourself. I thank God that I have always been a firm believer in helping other people in good, financially sound ways that do not create dependency.

Another reason I am working to teach other people how to make money is because I care about people. I have arrived at a place where I can help others, and I have a genuine and heartfelt concern for the well being of other people. Therefore, it is my calling and my pleasure to do what I can to help others learn what I know. After I help you become a millionaire, it is my hope that you will help someone else, and so on, and so on.

In my business, I meet people every day that should have more. And the only reason they do not have more is because they are not managing to the best potential what they do have. As the song says, "Them that's got shall get." The good news for you is that if you have *got* a job and are earning a living, then you have "got," and because of that, you can "get" more.

So, you have *got* a job, and now, you have *got* this book. Together, your job and this book can be used to implement a method of managing your money in a way that will make you a millionaire. Not withstanding all the late night TV talk shows that are constantly saying to you, "buy this or that tape, or come to this or that seminar, with no money, no nothing, and we will show you how to get rich overnight." I hope you do not fall for this, because instead of becoming rich, with most of these types of things, you are only becoming a sucker to make the pitchman or woman rich, or richer.

In this next section and in Chapter 1, I am going to talk to you about education. But before I get into this discussion, I want to tell you at the outset that my method can work for you whether or not you have a college degree. I am an advocate of education, and it is something that has greatly enhanced the quality of my life. So if you have a college degree, that's great. But I want to say to people who do not have a college degree that if you have a job, and if you are earning a living through your job, then you have "got," and you can still "get" more, with or without a college degree. My method is not about having a degree. It is about having the good sense and self-discipline you need to use and manage money wisely.

## Humble Beginnings—Up From Mississippi

When I was in junior high school it became clear to me that I would have to get away from the cotton fields of Prentiss, Mississippi in order to do something constructive with my life. That is when I became conscious of the importance of making good grades in school. You see, the only people I wanted to try to be like, and those who had jobs that impressed me, were college graduates. So to be like them, I needed to begin making good grades in school.

As a child, going to school impressed me that the learning process was fun. Therefore, school made a good impression on me. In fact, the principal of my elementary and middle school inspired me a lot, and other school leaders and teachers made a lasting impact on my life. Looking back, it is clear that I was blessed to have leaders of my grade school who truly cared about me and all the other students. One educator who left an indelible impression on my life was Professor J. E. Magee (or 'fessor Magee, as we called him). Mr. Magee was more than an educator; he taught me how to be a public speaker. In other words, he helped me develop a gift that has sustained me throughout my life. He inspired me to speak—to use my words and my voice to bring insight and understanding to others. Because of his inspiration, I competed in speaking competitions in school. When I was in the 8th grade, I went all the way to the national speaking competition sponsored by the Future Farmers of America organization (the FFA). In fact, that year I came in second in that national competition! My topic was "Keep Mississippi's Forests Green."

After graduating from high school, I chose to go to college. During my first three years at Alcorn College (now Alcorn State University) in Lorman, Mississippi, my goal was to become a chemistry teacher. I left college after three years to do a hitch in the army, however, and my thinking changed based on my experiences in the military. While working as an assistant to a major and to a lieutenant colonel (who were both astute investors in the stock market), I began to use my ability to save money to earn additional money by making loans (with interest) to other enlisted men. Therefore, my educational goals gradually shifted. The idea of making money had become more intriguing to me than studying chemistry. I found that money fascinated me, and I decided I wanted to become a banker.

My two-year hitch in the Army (and a visit back to where I spent two years before the army—Los Angeles) helped me decide that I would become a banker in the South. I made this decision because it appeared to me there were more opportunities available for blacks in the South.

I returned to Mississippi to complete my senior year of study, continuing my education at the University of Southern Mississippi in Hattiesburg. While there, I earned both undergraduate and graduate degrees in finance. After obtaining my M.B.A., I was ready to pursue my goal of becoming a banker, and of one day owning my own business.

I landed my first, and last, banking job in Dallas, Texas at Dallas Federal Savings and Loan. In 1972, I had packed my bags and with my wife and infant son headed for Dallas. Dallas Federal was offering me $850 a month for a position in real estate financing. The job was made more attractive by offering to assist my wife, Lela, in obtaining a position with the Dallas Independent School District. A graduate of Alcorn State University, Lela had worked as a schoolteacher in Mississippi while helping me attend graduate school.

When we moved to Dallas in 1972, all we owned was loaded into one small U-Haul trailer that we pulled to Dallas behind my 1968 Pontiac G.T.O. (that G.T.O. was fast). While in graduate school, our possessions included a mortgaged 80-acre tract of timberland in Mississippi that I purchased, and about $1,100. That's how we started our march toward financial freedom.

On my first Sunday night in Dallas, I met a man named A. A. Braswell at St. John Baptist Church. Mr. Braswell played a key role in altering the course of my life. We easily established a dialogue with each other because his wife was originally from Mississippi. The next night, Mr. Braswell took me to a meeting of the Dallas Black Chamber of Commerce. There I met Mr. C. A. Galloway, who would later become my partner and mentor in the real estate business.

After Mr. Galloway and I had known each other for a few months, he said to me, "Son, you are 28 years old. If by the time you're 40 you haven't made a million dollars, you ought to go back down to that farm in Mississippi." I agreed with him. I was prepared to go back if I had not accomplished that goal.

Mr. Galloway's challenge to me to become successful in business was more than just a statement in passing. Mr. Galloway believed it is important for blacks to be successful in business, and even more important for blacks to participate in the ownership of businesses. He also believed it is extremely important for the life of a black-owned business to continue after the original owner retires or dies. In other words, he believed in building wealth for generations to build upon, not just for one person or one family to enjoy.

After I had known Mr. Galloway for several years, he shared with me his long held dream of having a real estate business that would continue into perpetuity and grow stronger for future generations. He then invited me to join him in his real estate business. I did. I joined Mr. Galloway in his real estate business, but I joined for different reasons than those he had explained to me. I joined because by joining him in his business, I wouldn't have to start my own business from scratch, and I would be ahead of the game. That would enable me to get where I wanted to go faster. The organization he had built, and the good will he had developed, kept me from having to start at ground zero. So, although Mr. Galloway and I had different reasons for coming together, our coming together allowed both of us to accomplish our objectives.

Today, I am president and principal owner of Century 21 Galloway-Herron Realtors. The company has more than 60 associates and has grown to be the largest Century 21 office (by transactions) in the City of Dallas. The company has expanded its residential sales organization consisting of property management, commercial sales, consulting and a full service insurance.

At Century 21 Galloway-Herron we are constantly encouraging people to invest in real estate—and I practice what I preach. Therefore, my wife Lela and I own residential and commercial properties and timberland. Over the years, we have bought and sold properties of all types.

We meet people who think we have "made it" big, but I think our accomplishments have only touched the surface of the kind of success that is possible for us to have. However, when I think about what we have achieved, the truth probably lies somewhere between what I believe, and what others think.

*The Working Man and Woman's Guide To Becoming A Millionaire* is my plan detailing practical, guaranteed ways for everyday working-class people, like you and me, to attain financial success. I included myself in the last statement because this is actually the formula I've applied to my own life, and it has brought my family (and numerous other families) a great deal of financial success.

God has allowed me to acquire a level of wisdom and understanding that I am now able to share with you and millions of other people who are working hard, but who are still seeing very little in terms of financial gain. I want to help change this paradigm for the working class. I want people to understand that working for a living *can lead* to wealth, if they are willing to learn, and then to apply, a certain formula for success.

In 1988, I published my first book, *Ten Steps to Financial Freedom*. Much of the information contained in this book is the same as I spoke about in my first book. Yes—that's right. I wrote and distributed thousands of copies of a book similar to this one, and similar to other books written by other people since 1988, which have gone on to great publishing success. But I stand by my principles and my plan, and I'm presenting to you this 2006, revamped and updated version of what I know about how to use a job to become a millionaire. The reason I can present the same formula to you today is because my plan is based on financial principles that do not change. However, since times *do* change, I have integrated the same principles I discussed in my first book with new examples and explanations, and new information against the landscape of a new Millennium.

Much of the information contained within these pages, if put to use, will help you become successful in many aspects of your life. Still, the major emphasis—and the driving force—is on helping you to become financially independent. While it is true that what constitutes financial independence to one person may be considered poverty by another, my strategies will help you attain a level of financial literacy that will help you as you attempt to define financial freedom for yourself.

I define financial freedom as reaching the point in your life where your income from your investments, including your retirement fund, will support the lifestyle you desire without any additional work on your part. This has been my formula, and it is the same one I wrote about in the book I published back in 1988. Since that time, there have been many other wonderful books written by many brilliant people who are really presenting this same idea, using different words and in a different conceptual format.

I have done my best to make reading this book a pleasure, rather than a chore. In writing it, I have refrained from using highly technical terminology so that its lessons can speak to all kinds of people from all kinds of backgrounds. I want everyone—from the highly sophisticated and highly educated, to those preparing themselves for their first college degree, their first vocational training program, or their first job, to be able to follow my steps up the ladder to financial success. For this reason, this book includes every important factor I see as being related to obtaining this rare yet practical kind of success. It begins from the elementary steps of learning, training, and education, then advances to saving and investing, and graduates to deciding how your estate will be distributed after you die. All of these stages, I believe, are part of developing a "millionaire mindset"—part of learning how to have more. People who truly learn this lesson also cultivate a desire to leave something for the next generation. And that's real prosperity. That's real American progress.

In the first ten chapters, I have written about topics I have found to be absolutely essential to any discussion about becoming financially independent. Therefore, each chapter represents a vital step I recommend to help any working person gain the tools essential to achieving and sustaining financial freedom. The last three chapters represent some of the enduring beliefs I feel are critical to getting started and to staying the course as you work to create your own path to becoming a millionaire.

My final wish to you before you begin this journey is that after reading this book, you will "make haste while the sun is still shining" to start making a plan for your financial future. Don't waste precious time procrastinating, putting off for tomorrow what you can do today. The financial freedom you will gain on your way to becoming—and after becoming a millionaire—will keep you and/or your family safe and secure while you are still in the workforce, during retirement, and after you've gone from this life. My plan will teach you how to build an estate so you will be able to leave something worthwhile for your children and their children, and at the same time enhance the possibility of your memory staying alive into perpetuity. Remember the lesson of Proverbs 13:22, that "a good man leaveth an inheritance to his children's children."

*Step 1*

# Your Foundation:
# Education & Learning

1 I firmly believe that the only thing more important than education and learning, in life, is having God in your life. I also believe if you have God in your life, you will have the wisdom to know you need to seek education and learning. Proverbs 22: 6-7 says, "Train up a child in the way he should go. And when he is old he will not depart from it. The rich rule over the poor, and the borrower is servant to the lender."

Therefore, regardless of how you choose to pursue learning, I believe education is an invaluable resource that will help you in many ways, and no one will ever be able to take away from you all that education and learning can give to you. Education, therefore, is a wonderful way to invest today for a better tomorrow.

Knowledge is the precursor to everything. Since I know this to be the truth, building your foundation upon education and learning is the first step I am recommending to you on your path to becoming a millionaire. And even though you don't need a college degree to implement my method for becoming a millionaire, I am still recommending that you pursue education and learning passionately and enthusiastically, now and throughout your life. This is my recommendation for two main reasons:

1. Education/learning can help you become a self-disciplined, self-motivated thinker, better prepared to earn higher wages.
2. Education/learning can help you prepare your mind for making sound and wise decisions affecting the management and the

sustaining of your financial wealth, as well as decisions affecting the total quality of your life.

Education prepares you to compete in a competitive arena for jobs and other kinds of wealth-building opportunities. Lack of knowledge can render you unable to compete. The main reason this is true is that we live in what is often called the "Information Age." That means knowledge is a verifiable "commodity" that can make or break you. Getting an education prepares you for being able to continue your education and learning—on your own, long after you've matriculated through an organized program of study.

In the world economy, the financial well being of any nation is directly related to the education and training of its citizens. In the United States, the economic prosperity of a particular state, county, or city is directly linked to the population's levels of education. For example, in this country, the states with the lowest average levels of education among citizens also have some of the highest levels of poverty and financial strife. The same is true for individuals. On the average, the higher the education level, the more likely a person is to have a higher income level.

This also applies to households (single individual or family). The education and training of the primary breadwinner is the major determining factor of the household's standard of living. While there are always exceptions to any generalized rule, there is no denying that every individual *increases his or her chances* of becoming financially successful by getting an education or some form of specialized training.

I'm using education and training in the same context, but—of course, we know there is a difference between the two (I'll touch on this difference later in this chapter). The most important point I am making here, however, is that both education and training can prepare you for some type of work, and working for wages is the best way for the average person to begin a financial foundation leading to financial freedom.

In the past, just about every job required applicants to have at least a high school diploma. Today, more and more employers are requesting some college course work and/or a college degree for applicants to even be considered for certain jobs and positions. There are also many opportunities requiring advanced degrees, advanced training, licenses, and/or certifications. Therefore, it is a good idea for people who plan to attain financial freedom to prepare themselves through education and/or training going beyond the minimum requirements.

As I stated earlier, there are exceptions to any and every rule. You have probably heard about (or you might even know) individuals who have become extremely rich or very successful in life who dropped out of school, or who did not go to college. Let me assure you that these people, no matter who they are, are among the exceptions to the rule. Unless you are already sitting among the ranks of the exceptions (and if you are there's no need for you to read this book), it's probably not wise to expect to become one. It is much smarter to prepare yourself through education or training. After all, people often find their luck improves with preparation.

Too many people want to take "short cuts" to getting rich. That's why so many poor people are playing the lottery and going to the gambling joints, throwing good money away, hoping to hit it big. But all you have to do is to walk down the streets in Las Vegas, and look up and around you. That will tell who is winning at the gambling games, and it is not the masses of poor people. It would be much better to place your bets on education and training. This is something that will pay off in you becoming a more intelligent, learned person. And that is worth a lot—to you and to society in general.

## Starting Out With No Degree or Training?

This section of this chapter is for those people who have never attempted to obtain a degree or any type of training for a job or a career. If you (or your child) are still in high school, or you recently graduated from high school, you need to continue your education. Gone are the days when the high-school diploma represented the "end" of educational preparation. Today, it is more of a beginning than an ending. Let me encourage you now to continue your education beyond high school so that you can compete for higher-paying jobs.

Don't think that just because you know how to use a computer, you are automatically prepared to compete for higher-paying jobs. A lot of elementary schools today are preparing students using computers in the classroom, along with other kinds of the latest technologies. Still, the world is advancing so swiftly when it comes to technology, this kind of preparation is expected, and is no longer "exceptional." In other words, you must be technologically savvy just to keep pace in the Information Age. You need computer training in grade school to prepare you to use computers once you enter college or vocational training schools.

Most college degree programs now presume a certain level of computer competence, and they have developed curricula around that presumption. Students who have not attained this competence often find themselves needing "remedial" (correction of faulty study or faulty preparation) courses to bring them up to speed with the skills they need.

If you've never thought about going to college, you need to do some research to find out about your options. You might be eligible for financial aid, or you might qualify for student loans that can help pay for your college education. There are many books that can help you get started on the path to obtaining a college degree or vocational training: From deciding what to study to finding ways to pay for your education. Some of these books are included at the end of this chapter on a list of resources for people interested in furthering or continuing their education.

If you have not already done so, I strongly encourage you to get started on your education. Learning is, and always will be, the first and most crucial step on any path to financial freedom.

No matter how many people you see becoming successful based on winning the lottery, being discovered by Hollywood, becoming a rap, hip-hop, R & B, or rock star, or any other of a multitude of occurrences resulting from talent, skill, or just plain old good luck—if I were you, I'd still place my bet on education. Even stars benefit from learning and training.

I realize that a lot of people are using models for financial success these days that don't involve going to college or working for a lifetime in one job or one career area. Still, the average person in America needs to work for a living. And people who need to work for a living need to prepare themselves by becoming educated. Even those who become successful through talent or luck still need an education base from which to build. When I was a child, there was a saying that "a fool and his money are soon parted." I believe it is the lack of education, learning, and wisdom that separates many people from their newly acquired wealth when they bypass the education process on the way to fame and fortune.

Therefore, even though I have told you my method can be implemented by anyone willing to work, with or without a college degree, I still am an advocate of education. I believe you will enjoy your success, and your life, a lot more when you have the kind of knowledge and understanding that can only be gained by going through some kind of education process.

## Did You Get Your Degree or Training a Long Time Ago?

If you obtained your college degree or training many years ago (ten or more), and you still have not attained financial freedom, you might benefit from taking "refresher" courses, or from obtaining an advanced degree, or more and/or different training. This is an important consideration if you find yourself "stuck" where you are right now. You might have tried to get a better job or a promotion on your current job, only to find the better jobs and promotions are going to people who have attained higher levels of education and/or training. If this is the case, there is no time like now to begin making yourself more marketable.

I've heard people say such silly things as: "I'm too old to go back to school. Why, I'll be 39, or I'll be 40 years old in a few months!" Well, my question is: How old are you going to be if you don't go back to school? In my opinion, when you are poor *and* uneducated, you are going to look older than you really are, anyway. It seems to me that—on the average—people who know more learn how to care for themselves and their health better than people who are uneducated.

The point I'm making here is that it doesn't matter how old you are if you are fed-up with the standard of living you now have, and you want to make a change for the better. You're going to be the same age (if you keep living) whether you're in school learning something new, or not in school, accepting the status quo for your life.

Today, there are technological advancements allowing adults to go to school or learn without leaving home (distance education). Therefore, you should look into both traditional (classroom environment) and non-traditional education alternatives (online and weekend education and training).

You may be someone from the "Baby Boom" generation who is no longer "young" and needing a first degree, but you're not "old" either. You might be in that adult "tween" stage of life when you could get a second degree, a master's or greater, go for training in another career area, or obtain some type of certification allowing you to transition into a new or better career (or get a promotion at your current place of employment).

There are books that can help you get started on the path to obtaining additional or advanced degrees or training. Some of these books are included among resources listed at the end of this chapter.

Let me urge you to stop procrastinating, and to get started on augmenting your education. After all, if you have not attained—and you strongly feel you will not attain—financial freedom on the path you're now following, you're going to have to do something different. It is said that the best way to keep getting what you've always gotten is to keep doing what you've always done. It is also said that to keep doing the same thing over and over, and expecting a different result, is the definition of a fool. Therefore, if you want to see things change in your life for the better, you're going to have to do something different. A new path is waiting for you. I hope you will begin today your walk towards the kind of financial freedom that can make you a millionaire.

## The Difference Between Education and Training

What does a college degree offer that vocational training does not? Why should a person choose one path over the other? Without getting too "in-depth," the main difference has to do with the desired end result.

A college education, usually, provides a broad base of knowledge presented in the form of concepts, theories, principles, and ideas with the goal of preparing people who want or need to recall facts and apply concepts. This foundation of theories and concepts provide the degree holder with a set of functional "thinking skills" allowing them to gain even greater knowledge by continuing their education (through work experience or further education). While colleges and universities might prepare people to work in a particular area or field, they don't usually focus on preparing people for a particular job. Their main goal is to "educate" for enlightenment and increased understanding.

People who obtain a college degree from one school can usually continue their education at another school, building upon their knowledge base. For example, you might obtain a bachelor's degree at one school, and go to a completely different school for your master's degree. Or, you might begin a bachelor's degree at one school, then transfer to another school to complete your degree. You can do this because traditional educational institutions in the United States—in general—have similar educational standards and degree requirements.

Vocational training, instead of providing a broad base of knowledge, focuses on one skill or a set of specific skills with the goal of enabling a person to do a particular job in a specific type of workplace. Usually, the preparation you receive through one vocational school is not transferable to other institutions. That means if you study to become a barber, or a computer repair technician, if you one day decide you want to also obtain a traditional college degree—often, the courses you took for your vocational preparation will not "transfer" as course requirements for your college degree.

Vocational training is usually completed in less time than it takes to obtain a college degree. The typical college degree takes four years of study, while vocational training usually takes two years or less (depending on the skill being learned).

Whether you choose education or training is up to you, and should be based on your interests and goals. Either path can lead to financial freedom. Either path can pave the way for you to implement my plan for becoming a millionaire. After all, there are barbers and cosmetologists who have opened up multiple shops and have become millionaires. There are vocationally trained nurses and medical technicians whose work allows them to earn six-figure incomes after many years of work experience.

There are many different paths to education and training in the marketplace today. If you're considering education, it would be a good idea to spend some thinking about your interests and talents, and some time reading about and comparing what kinds of jobs and money-making possibilities are offered by different work and/or career paths.

**Books and Other Resources for Traditional and Non-Traditional Continuing or Advanced Education**
(These listings do not constitute any endorsement of any school, vocational program, or training or certification program.)

_The Truth About Getting In : A Top College Advisor Tells You Everything You Need to Know_ by Katherine Cohen, Ph.D., April, 2002

_How to Earn a College Degree: When You Think You Are Too Old, Too Busy, Too Broke and Too Scared_ by E. Faith Ivery and Sharon Kirk (August 2003)

_But What If I Don't Want to Go to College? A Guide to Success Through Alternative Education_ by Harlow Giles Unger (Sept. 1998)

_Losing The Race : Self-Sabotage in Black America_ by John McWhorter August, 2000 (This book offers an interesting perspective on education and career underachievement.)

_College Board Scholarship Handbook 2003_ by The College Board (A guide to over 2,300 scholarships, internships, and loan programs for undergraduates.)

_Guide to Distance Learning Programs 2003 (Peterson's Guide to Distance Learning Programs, 2003)_ by Petersons Publishing

_Bears' Guide to Earning Degrees by Distance Learning_ by John Bear, Mariah Bear

_Internet Web Site_: Visit www.all-college-degrees.com to search by job category or state for college degrees and vocational preparation in just about any field.

*Summary of Step 1*
## Build on a Foundation of Learning

The first step is to build your life on a learning foundation. You should learn to love and appreciate learning, because it is absolutely crucial to finding your way to financial freedom. Never shy away from an opportunity to learn something of value. Be a sponge for information. Learning is not painful; it's something you can enjoy. Begin to cherish knowledge, so that you can use it to help yourself more in all aspects of your life. This book is packed with information meant to guide you, effortlessly, down the path to financial independence. Therefore, you should exercise your new enjoyment of learning as you read and absorb the elements of this plan for helping you become a millionaire.

# Never Run Out of Money

2

I heard a story once about this man who was well known—some giant of industry—who was to be the keynote speaker at a highly attended finance-related convention. Everyone was elated that the organizers had secured such a wise speaker, for the man was truly a legend in his own time. Everyone was prepared to hang on his every word, and to take copious notes that would surely be of interest to their office colleagues and people unable to attend the gathering. As the man was introduced people applauded, giving him a loud standing ovation. The crowd settled down as the admired speaker prepared to open his mouth. Looking out over the crowded room, the man knew he had the complete attention of his audience. He then gave his speech. He said, "Never run out of money." Then he sat down. That was his speech.

And that's essentially what I am saying to you in this chapter: Never run out of money. Now that you're committed to increasing your level of education and knowledge, and to becoming more enthusiastic about learning, now it's time to make sure that when you begin making more money, you'll know what to do with it. If you're serious about finding your way to millions—and about maintaining millionaire status once you arrive there—then you'll learn to appreciate the value of that speaker's words, and you'll never run out of money.

In fact, if my plan is to work for you, you *have* to make sure that you never run out of money. Why? Because you cannot invest in anything if you have no money. People who understand the need to save know that it is not good to run out of money. There is no magic in finding a way to never run out of money. There is only one way, and that is to keep some of the money you earn. I'll say it again. The only way to make sure you don't run out is to put some away. When you manage to do this, you can always get more. People who have money can get money, while people who don't have money cannot.

Therefore, never let yourself run out of money. Keep some of your money, and you will be able to build your assets and make financial plans for the future. Understand that this second step in my plan for your financial freedom is crucial. It is also very simple. In fact, it's so simple that you may say it is nothing new. No matter what you have to say about it or what you may think about it, Step 2 of my plan is STILL a simple recommendation that you begin saving at least 10% of all you earn. That's it. I want you to save 10% of what you bring home every month as income.

Doing this one simple thing, month after month, will *guarantee* that you can be well on your way toward becoming a millionaire.

Almost every self-made, financially independent person you can talk to will tell you that you should pay yourself first in an amount that you can afford and in an amount that you can keep up, all your working life. I strongly believe that a person's future financial success is directly related to how well he or she follows this simple principle of saving.

## Put Your Savings on "Cruise Control"

Saving is the one step in my plan that you cannot skip or go around. It is the pivotal point of the whole plan to lock down financial freedom for you and your family. It is absolutely the best way for men and women who must work to earn a living, to insure that they will never run out of money. Therefore, to make sure that you implement this important step, you should strongly consider taking the responsibility for saving out of your own hands. How? Put it on automatic pilot, or "cruise control."

When you put the responsibility for saving on cruise control, your financial institution—and not you—will take care of putting your money into a savings account. If you work for an employer, you can have the money automatically withdrawn and placed in savings through your company's credit union, if you are a member. Or, you can set up an automatic draft through your bank, so that after your paycheck is deposited, the bank automatically puts a specified amount into your savings account.

For the self-employed, you should do what I do. That is, have the money for your savings program automatically charged to a credit card (I use my American Express card) each month. I choose American Express because if you pay your balance each month, no interest is charged.

Whether you use a credit card or have the money automatically deducted by your employer or a financial institution, the point is you must make saving money a habit. You must take it out of your own hands, and make it an involuntary action. You have to find a way to put your savings program on "cruise control," so that you leave "driving" the plan to devices other than yourself. I am completely convinced this is the *absolute best way* to insure that it is done every month, without fail.

### Pay Yourself First, Every Payday

The opposite of saving 10% or some significant portion of what you earn is spending or consuming everything you earn. No matter how small or how large your income, you should be able to save at least 10% of it. Instead of eating out often, or instead of buying material goods that you really don't need, you should instead put that money away for yourself.

For those of you who are currently paying out more than you earn, and are borrowing to pay bills, the formula still applies with some variation.

First, you should set aside 10% of your take home pay for savings. Second, you will need to make a list of all your debts. And, finally, you should complete a list of budget items necessary for living your life. Remember, you only need to budget your living expenses, and not your other debts. Now, subtract the total of your budget from your income *after* your savings have been deducted. The amount that remains will be all you have left for your debts.

Whatever you have left, you will divide among your creditors. Believe me, your creditors would rather that you give them something every month, rather than nothing. Therefore, you will need to call, write, or e-mail each one of your creditors so that you and they can work out a repayment plan for your debts, based on the amount of money you have left after subtracting your living expenses, your savings, and your giving. Your creditors will be glad to know you have included paying them in your new budget, and once you begin using your savings to secure investments, and are earning from your investments, you can pay off some or all of these creditors.

Included next is a sample budget illustrating the "pay yourself first" savings principle.

## Pay Yourself First Monthly Budget Example

| | |
|---|---|
| **TAKE-HOME PAY** | **$4,000** |
| Pay Yourself/SAVE | 10% = $400 |
| Charity/Tithe | 10% = $400 |
| **Available for Living Expenses** | **$3,200** |
| **LIVING EXPENSES** | |
| Mortgage Payment | $1100 |
| Utilities | $300 |
| Groceries | $325 |
| Auto Maintenance & Gas | $160 |
| Insurance | $200 |
| Miscellaneous | $250 |
| **Total Expenses** | **$2,335** |
| **Total remaining for Debts** | **$865** |
| **DEBTS** | |
| Car Note | $550 |
| Credit Cards | $125 |
| Department Stores | $75 |
| Discretionary | $115 |
| **Total Debt** | **$865** |
| **Total Expenditures** | **$3,200** |

Now, if it is easier or more advantageous for you to earn more income than it is for you to negotiate your debt, then feel free to supplement your income (through a part-time job of some sort) to the extent that it will allow you to save at least 10%. Ideally, you should lower your expenses and increase your income at the same time.

Let us imagine a 35-year old man or woman who, tomorrow, will begin to save $100 per month.

Assume that this person's savings will earn 9% compounded annually. At the end of the 30th year, or on his or her 65th birthday, this person will have $178,290 in cash. Not a bad birthday gift, and not a bad "nest egg" for retirement. And if this person can manage to double or triple their savings now, he or she will double or triple the size of their "nest egg." It should become easier to increase your savings amount, as you grow older. Why? Because most of the time income increases as time goes by (with raises and/or job promotions or advancement). For many people, after age 45, expenses should decrease (with children becoming self-supporting adults).

Now put yourself into the picture. See and feel yourself in possession of the money you are going to have at retirement. See yourself at retirement traveling, fishing, hunting, relaxing worry-free, or doing whatever you enjoy doing. If you can see yourself doing these things, it will help make it much easier for you to save. You'll be thankful that you won't have to pick up aluminum cans in the summer heat or winter cold to make ends meet at age 65 or 75.

Look at the chart on the next page. Since we don't know what will be the actual rate of interest you will earn over all those years, the chart will show some alternatives of what $100 per month, compounded at various rates of interest, will earn for you. The interest rate over the period from 2001 to 2006 has been extremely low. In fact, it has set a record low. Therefore, we cannot use one or two past years as in our example. Instead, we must look at the historical rates to project to the future. Since no one can say with certainty what the rates will be, we will take a long view and use interest rates from 3% to 12%. The Savings Chart shows the amount of savings accumulated at $100 per month in 5-year intervals, up to 30 years using interests rates of 3%, 5%, 8%, 10% and 12%.

## Savings Chart (saving $100 a month)

| Interest Rate | 5th Year | 10th Year | 15th Year | 20th Year | 25th Year | 30th Year |
|---|---|---|---|---|---|---|
| 3% | 6,488 | 14,009 | 22,754 | 32,912 | 44,712 | 58,419 |
| 5% | 6,828 | 15,592 | 26,840 | 41,274 | 59,799 | 83,527 |
| 8% | 7,403 | 18,774 | 35,188 | 59,307 | 95,736 | 146,815 |
| 10% | 7,059 | 21,037 | 41,940 | 75,602 | 129,818 | 217,131 |
| 12% | 8,538 | 23,866 | 50,103 | 99,914 | 189,763 | 352,991 |

Do this for me. Get a pen and a piece of paper and write this down: "I will pay (write in your name) the first of each month not less than 10% of my earnings. No matter how large or small my income, I will save at least 10% of my income, starting with my next paycheck."

## Developing a Savings Habit

Many years ago, I read a book by George S. Clason titled *The Richest Man in Babylon*. In this book, Clason points out the wisdom of saving and investing in your own future. The main idea of the book is about one man's (Algamish's) answer to another man's (Arkad's) question about how the first man became wealthy. Algamish's answer is what I consider to be the real cornerstone of wealth. He told Arkad that a part of everything he earned was his to keep. In other words, he was saying PAY YOURSELF FIRST.

Most of us have no problem trying to pay the baker, the butcher, the barber, the candlestick maker, the auto finance companies and department stores, and others every month. And most of us then have nothing left for ourselves. But if you are going to develop a savings habit—if you are going to make it part of your personality; part your daily "attitude" about your life, then you must learn to reverse the order of what you are doing with your money. When it comes to your income, you should be getting the top take for your savings.

When we attend church on Sunday, we are told to pay God. That's fine. I support tithing, and I pay my tithe. At least 10% of my income goes to my church and other charitable causes. But remember that the Bible says, "Love thy neighbor as thyself" (Leviticus 19:18; Leviticus 19:34; Matthew 19:19; Matthew 22:39; Mark 12:31; Luke 10:27; Romans 13:9; Galatians 5:14; and James 2:8). This statement presumes, however, that love for self comes first. It means that Christ thought we should first love ourselves. When Christ says, "Love thy neighbor as thyself", it has meaning only if you love yourself. Therefore, even God expects you to look out for yourself before you look out for any other mortal being. Therefore, what I am recommending for you is in keeping with Biblical thought. Looking out and caring for you is the best way to show your love for you. God loves you, and I believe He expects you to love you too. So learn to look out for yourself and your family as God's children.

I realize there are a lot of working people who don't earn a lot of money. But there are almost no cases where a person who's working can't manage to save some money. Maybe he or she can't save as much as the next person, but I don't believe that there are many people who can't save something. Any person who is serious about becoming a millionaire must find a way to save something from every single paycheck, whether it's 20%, 10%, 5%, or 2%. If you have to, start by saving whatever you can. Then, as you learn to manage your finances better, work up to saving at least 10% of your income, and more if you can. You must learn to take your savings off the top! Before paying anybody else, pay yourself. Don't leave the option to save or not to save up to you. Take it out of your own hands, and make it an involuntary action. Use the "cruise control" method I spoke of earlier in this chapter. Start your savings program by putting the money you save into a saving's account so that it will begin to accrue interest as soon as possible.

Success in a savings program depends on your ability to develop a "savings habit." If you are successful in your savings program and are able to develop a savings habit, you will be giving a big boost to your plan of one day becoming a millionaire. However, developing a savings habit is just the beginning of your savings program. You must also be disciplined enough to protect your savings and not spend it at the first opportunity you get to buy something new. And you must have the self-discipline and personal resolve to not spend it just to satisfy spending "impulses," or to satisfy your immediate and unnecessary wants or desires.

As a new "Saver," as you watch your savings grow, you will most likely be tempted to spend it. You may even manage to convince yourself that it's all right to withdraw just a small amount of interest since this may be viewed as "extra money." But listen to this: If you are *ever* going to reach your financial goals, you should not spend the interest earned on your savings and you should let the principal (the non-interest money you are putting into the savings account) remain intact. In fact, you should never use the principal.

In the book *The Richest Man in Babylon* the process of using the interest that you've earned is referred to as "eating up the offspring." If you are able to develop the savings habit and can start earning interest from the money you've saved, the earned interest will make your savings pool build into a significant amount. The moment you start to use the interest it is the equivalent of a cattle rancher selling or slaughtering all the beautiful offspring that are born to his livestock, instead of using them to produce a larger herd. Spend the money your money earns, and you'll find yourself wondering, "Where's the beef?" before too long!

The Ford Foundation provides a classic example demonstrating how using money to grow money can result in an extremely large amount of cash being earned. According to a 2002 article in the *Chronicle of Philanthropy*, in 1991 the Foundation's assets that were $6.1 billion, by 2002, had climbed to $11.3 billion.

Another example is the many endowments that fund colleges and universities across the country. When looking at the savings habits of some of the rich families of our nation—like the Rockefellers, we can see that they set up trust funds that never become smaller than the principal used to set up the fund. This is true because the principal is protected, and the recipients of those funds are only allowed to use the interest earned. And in many cases, they are only allowed to use a percentage of the interest earned, and all the while the fund grows larger and larger. Now, I don't want to hear you say "I don't have those big sums of money so I can't do that." Don't say that, and don't even think it, because the same principle applies to one dollar as it does to one million dollars. The only difference is in how many zeros are added to the amount.

The cardinal rule to follow is never use the principal of your savings plan.

In the book *The Richest Man in Babylon*, after a year had passed, Algamish returned to see if Arkad had been able to save one-tenth of his earnings. Arkad had indeed been able to save one-tenth of his earnings with no problem at all.

Algamish then requested to know what Arkad had done with the money he saved. Arkad told him he had given the money to a brick maker who was traveling the far seas to purchase rare jewels for him to resell at higher prices.

This angered Algamish who scolded Arkad for giving his money to someone who knew nothing about making money, and Algamish assured Arkad that his money was surely lost.

When the brick maker returned, he had been sold glass instead of rare jewels. Arkad had entrusted his money to someone who knew nothing about rare jewels and the brick maker had lost his money. Arkad had learned a valuable lesson. He would trust his savings only with those experienced in such matters.

The lesson of this part of the story is "Do not gamble with the money you save." Always put your savings in a safe place over which *you* have control. When you have accumulated enough to invest (and obviously, I think real estate is the place for you to invest), invest only in something about which you are knowledgeable and over which you have control. Select something that is going to bring you a return on your investment. Unlike the young man in Clason's book, never give your money to anyone or listen to anyone who has no knowledge or experience in the particular area of investment you choose.

The key is to start a savings program now. Continue to save even after you have accumulated enough savings for investments. Another key point to follow is to save all of your working life while you have an income.

Saving money is something I learned from my parents. And I promise, if you learn to follow this plan, you will find that although you cannot save your way to super wealth, you can save enough to get started so that you can invest your way to super wealth.

You might be wondering, "What if I have a real emergency? Should I use the money then?" In the case of a real emergency, the smart thing to do is to borrow! You're better off to borrow the money even if you have to use the savings as collateral. You're likely to pay back the loan, and *you'll* still have your savings! That is one of the secrets to accumulating wealth. Having something in the bank makes it possible for you to get money on credit. For this reason, you should never use your savings. This principle is not something that's complicated, and you don't have to be very smart to see the beauty of it. The real issue is that all of us have a tendency to not follow through on our savings goals, and we are likely to want to spend our hard-earned money on some consumer item that is probably worthless in the great scheme of things.

The minute I started to work, I began saving money from every paycheck. I had the money automatically drafted out of my checking account into my savings. I would not trust myself because I knew I might find a good reason this month or the next month not to make that deposit into my savings. Even today, I authorize the drafting of a certain amount out of my checking account to go into my savings.

## Saving Through an Insurance Policy

In the past, most of us, if we did manage to develop a savings habit, simply placed our money in a bank or a savings and loan, and some even stuffed their money into the mattress (not recommended). In these cases the return on the money was very small (or nonexistent in the case of the mattress!) It only provided enough protection for simple emergencies. A family—a mother, father, and children—is doing itself a disservice if the parents don't take a look at other kinds of savings programs. With a good savings program, you're able to get more than one thing accomplished.

We have two primary economic problems we are faced with that affect our families that we can do something about. The two problems are: (1) we could live too long, and (2) we could die too soon.

In the event we're faced with problem number 1, we've lived past the capability of our resources to take care of us. That means we've lived too long. If we encounter problem number 2, that means we've died before accomplishing our financial goals. In effect, we have died too soon.

Neither of these problems has to happen. With insurance, we can guarantee that neither will happen. Just because one dies does not mean he or she is automatically relieved of the financial responsibility of taking care of a family. There was a time when this responsibility was strictly the domain of the husband, but now the dollar is so cheap and it takes so much money to live, and wages are so low that—generally, both husband and wife have to work. Therefore, both husband and wife must share in the financial responsibility of the family. If either happens to "kick the bucket" early, he or she is not relieved of this responsibility, especially if children have been brought into the world, and they are not yet adults.

This premature death business is taken care of through life insurance. If you calculate that it will take $250,000, $500,000, $750,000 or even $1,000,000 to carry out your financial responsibility in your absence, then all you have to do is buy a life insurance policy for that amount. It's just that simple. If you should die prematurely, that money will be there to take care of your children in the same manner as before your death, and it will pay for their living expenses and their education. I believe that one of the reasons that too many people of my race, the African American people, are poor—and why each generation seems to get poorer and poorer—is that almost everybody has to start out in life at ground zero.

Starting at zero today puts you below where your father or mother started. The truth of the matter is, sometimes we start so low that we might have to look up to see the bottom. There is no reason why this should be the case, however, because anyone with a sustainable income can afford insurance. It's not that difficult to discipline yourself by budgeting for an insurance policy.

If you take out a policy and die before you're old enough to retire, or before your financial obligations are discharged, then that insurance will take care of your obligations. I don't really know of anything else that will take care of that responsibility for you. Of course, if you happen to inherit a lot of money or accumulate a lot of money from some other source, that money would be available to provide for your family in your absence. Should you die early, that money can substitute for insurance. But I don't know many of us who can count on that kind of occurrence.

Now that we've looked at insurance as a way to take care of the family if we should die prematurely, next, we need to look at the other side of this coin: living past your resources.

Are you aware that only about three percent of Americans who reach the age of 65 are financially independent? That means those who are not financially independent are dependent upon others. In fact, more than 30% of Americans who reach age 65 are totally dependent on somebody else, whether it's the government or their family, to take care of them financially.

The tragedy is that the trend towards financial dependency in old age is continuing. And you should realize that if you keep living, one day it's going to happen to you too, unless you do something now to make sure that it does not. You don't have to be a genius to comprehend this. In fact, you probably know somebody close to you, or in your family, who turned 65, was poor, broke, destitute, and wasn't able to take care of himself. If you look in your own family, it might be your mother, father, cousin, or uncle. But take a look, and I promise you, you'll find somebody who has reached that age, and is financially dependent on somebody else, or who is living in poverty. Keep looking, and I promise you, you will find him or her.

Now what makes you think it's not going to happen to you? If it has happened to all these other people, why isn't that same thing going to happen to you? Believe me, just as day follows night and vice versa, it is inevitable, if you keep living, that one day you are going to have to stop working. If you continue to live, it is inevitable that you are going to need an alternative source of money, because your job will no longer be there. You might have a pension, but it is probably not going to be enough to take care of your expenses. Therefore, you and you alone, should take control of the situation now, while you are fit and able to work and save. The government is not going to be of much help to you in your old age. So please don't be counting on Social Security to save you. It won't.

Social Security may be broke and out of business before it's time for you to begin collecting from it. The way the federal government is running up debt at an all-time high in 2005, the Social Security system may be out of business in the not-so-distant future.

I've even heard talk about them increasing the age at which people can become eligible to start drawing a check from Social Security. Increasing the age? I heard comedian Chris Rock on television one night telling a joke about this very thing. He argued that the age of eligibility for social security should be lowered to about age 35 for black men, so that we can get some of our money back.

In Dallas, Texas, I come across too many people, and I know far too many people, who can barely pay the utility bills. How do we manage the side of the coin that I call living too long? If you take care of dying too soon through the use of life insurance, and put your money into a saving program or some type of whole life policy, this will make it easy for you to take care of living too long as well.

The important point here is to buy life insurance with a face value large enough that upon your death, the proceeds will take care of your family. Also, save a sufficient amount of cash in an insurance policy, IRA, savings account or any similar method to have income when you retire to maintain your living standard.

These plans works well for people who are seeking long term cash value growth they can use to save for retirement, fund their children's college education, purchase a new home, or pay for a vacation. Essentially, there are three strategies for investing in life insurance. The choice of strategy should be based upon whether you want it for financial protection, investments, or both. In either case, a universal life program is an outstanding one.

Let me tell you one other good point about the life products with a savings feature. The money you earn with them IS NOT TAXABLE. You have to pay taxes on the interest paid to you at a savings and loan, or at a bank. On any life insurance policy, and especially the universal life insurance program, the inside cash build-up that you are earning by virtue of interest is not taxable until such time as you start to withdraw that money. By then you should be in a lower tax bracket, so you have a double advantage. First of all, you get paid a higher rate of interest while the money is building, and, since it's not taxable, it builds up faster.

If you consistently put money into the insurance policy as a way to provide for your family, at age 65, you could have $50,000, $100,000, or $200,000 available for retirement, depending on how much you decide to put into it now and in the future. So you can see that today, the insurance policy is no longer a luxury. It's a form of saving and investing. Not only can it be a very good investment, it is also a very good way for you to be financially responsible. There is, of course, the idea made famous by A. L. Williams. He advocated buying term life and investing the difference. Mr. Williams is correct in that you can buy only term life insurance and invest all the savings from buying term insurance. There is just one problem, however. People will not invest the difference.

For the person who owns his or her business, the business can buy the insurance policy. In that way, the business owner has use of that money before it is taxed. Dollars from the business can buy the policy and there are no taxes paid on the income that's being used. The policy can accrue until such time as a person retires, and at 60 or 65 years of age, he can start to withdraw money from it. If the policyholder should die prematurely, the proceeds from the insurance policy are not taxable.

I hope I've explained this well enough for you to see that while developing the habit of saving money by putting it in the bank (or wherever you want to save it) is a wonderful thing to do, it is also good to explore other kinds of investments. The whole life, universal life and annuity insurance programs are forms of investment that include all of the major factors and benefits you need from a savings program. They offer savings, protection, and future income to help you move confidently toward financial freedom.

Another important feature of these policies is that you can borrow money from the cash build-up. Well, you don't really borrow the money as such. It really continues to grow. Instead, you borrow from the company. The insurance company will let you have any amount that's equivalent to your cash build-up. Then, you pay that back with interest, but your cash keeps building. Actually, if necessity dictates, you can withdraw the money. So, this kind of insurance is totally flexible, and totally liquid to you at all times. Under these programs, if you do withdraw all your cash, you still maintain your life insurance coverage.

The practical thing to do is to borrow the money and pay it back as soon as you can. If you should die before paying back all that you have borrowed, the amount still owed would be deducted from the death benefits.

There are other kinds of saving-through-investment programs in the marketplace that may fit some individuals even better than this type of insurance policy. The individual who buys only term insurance, or an individual who is not in the position to buy insurance because of health or others reasons, should have an investment and savings program that will meet his or her needs. If you decide to go this route, look for an "investment type person" to help you, or a good financial planner. Find someone knowledgeable in all areas of wealth and financial planning to give you advice on alternatives best matching your needs. It is essential that you have some kind of saving-through-investment program providing for *you* if you live too long, and for *your family* if you die too soon.

I hope this chapter has helped you come to the realization that you have to start one or more savings programs to insure yourself, and (if you have one) your family's future. It is easier to do than you think. Just as you don't question yourself when you want to make some type of "impulse" purchase as you're waiting in the checkout line at the grocery store, or at some discount outlet, don't question yourself when it's time to take money form your check, and put it into your savings account.

From every job that I've ever had, I've saved money. Before I ever came to Dallas, I had managed to save a little money. When I was in the army, I saved my money. As a private, I was probably making about $116 a month, but before I left the army in 1967, I had a couple thousand dollars saved. Can you imagine that? I had the military draft the money out of my paycheck. So as far back as my military career, I managed to save. Therefore, I've known for a long time that a savings program is absolutely essential if you expect to ever become rich as a working person.

## Summary of Step 2
### Put Your Savings on Cruise Control

Putting your savings program on "cruise control" allows you to begin seeing your way clear to realizing true financial freedom. When you put your savings on cruise control, your financial independence will move closer and closer to you—and not farther and farther away, as will happen without a good savings plan. Using cruise control, you will have money to make investments, as long as you continue to save. As you refine this habit, you will begin to feel the power, confidence, and peace of mind that comes along with feeling more financially secure. Believe me, it's a great feeling.

*Step 3*

# Increase Your Earning Power
# with the Right "Work Attitude"

3 Over the years, I have been taught to work hard. As a child, I saw my father being hard-working and dedicated to running a farm and a general country store. I grew up knowing the value of hard work. I've also read numerous publications and books where the authors point out that the more effort you put into your work, the luckier you become, and the more rewards seem to come your way.

In the Old Testament, Proverbs 22:2 says: "The rich and poor have this in common, the Lord is the maker of them all." That says to me we are all capable of achieving and accomplishing. We have a common Caretaker, who does not care for one more than the other. In fact, the only thing that separates us from our potential for achievement, as far as I am concerned, is our beliefs and our attitude about work.

I firmly believe it is very important *never* to do the least amount of work you can on a particular job. I believe it is *always* important to do more than is expected of you. Remember this: The attitude that is going to sustain you on the path to financial freedom is not one molded in mediocrity. Doing "just enough to get by" is not honorable, and it is not going to get you far from the starting gate on the path to financial independence.

For this reason, I am urging you to develop an attitude of doing more than is expected of you. As you do your work every day, become self-motivated to achieve. You shouldn't need a supervisor breathing down your neck to make you want to do more. Your self-respect should empower you to do more. And you should begin every job you ever accept with this attitude.

You should form a habit of working to your maximum potential (as opposed to a habit of doing the least amount of work possible) for the maximum number of dollars.

If you allow yourself to develop the bad habit of doing the least amount of work possible, it will be hard for you to change—even if you somehow manage to start your own business one day. An attitude of mediocrity spells sure and certain defeat. This is true because by allowing your mind to accept less than you are capable of doing, you are permitting yourself to become indoctrinated with "skating" and "getting by." Once this becomes ingrained as part of your character, it will be very hard to alter this bad habit, and it will follow you into many different aspects of your life. It will follow you into your marriage, into caring for your children and other loved ones, and so forth and so on. Following that faulty principle, you will most likely not have sustained success in business, or in life.

Whether or not you know it, when you begin to practice doing more, you greatly increase your chances of being rewarded on your job with promotions and increased pay. More importantly, doing more than is expected of you requires that you use your specialized knowledge to make greater and greater accomplishments, and you will undoubtedly become more valuable in the work you are doing. Even if the company employing you does not recognize this by rewarding you with promotions and/or increased pay, you are still becoming better prepared to market your skills to other companies. Therefore, it is truly a *win-win* proposition to personally reject mediocre performance (from you), and to adopt an attitude of doing more.

If you happen to be in a job that does not motivate you to excel and to give your best, then you need to seriously consider changing jobs. You should seek work that challenges you to learn and grow in your skill area or in your field of interest. Remember, knowledge (in and of itself) is no good. But knowledge is good, powerful, and of great economic benefit *if you can put it to use.*

Increase your earning power on a job by doing more than expected. Doing this will enable you to become more knowledgeable and more marketable, professionally. By becoming a specialist in what you do, you're also preparing yourself to one day sell your services as proprietor of your own business. When others begin to look to you for certain knowledge, your earning potential increases tremendously. According to Proverbs 15:19, "The way of the lazy man is like a hedge of thorns but the way of the righteous is made plain." In other words, when you are lazy, you are your primary hindrance. On the other hand, when you are not lazy—or when you are smart or active—you become your primary help. You become sought after for your knowledge and abilities, and you become more valuable to yourself.

## The Value of Positive Thinking

In 1960, I entered Alcorn State University, then known as Alcorn College. I remained there three years before going into the Army. As I've stated earlier in this book, after getting out of the Army I finished school at the University of Southern Mississippi.

As a college graduate with an advanced degree, I've read many books for school and even more just for knowledge. Of all the books I've read in my life, one of the few that made a lasting impression on me is *The Power of Positive Thinking* by Dr. Norman Vincent Peale. Many of his ideas about the importance of the link between positive thinking and enjoying a happy and successful life made a profound impact on me, and I have internalized them as part of my own belief system.

I know today that positive thinking was part of my lifestyle before I ever read even one word of Dr. Peale's book. But it was not until after I had read the book that I began to think of myself as a positive thinker. Now I realize that before reading the book, I was simply not mature enough to realize *I was already a positive thinker*. Reading his eloquently spoken and memorable words just made me recognize the powerful force I'd had inside of me all along—my natural or God-given tendency to be a positive thinker.

One thing in the book that made me believe wholeheartedly in Dr. Peale's ideas about positive thinking was the fact that he believed strongly in the power of prayer. Since I also believed strongly in this power, I felt that Dr. Peale and I actually shared many common and important beliefs. In addition to his stance on the importance of prayer, the book also presented many other arguments, statements, and points that were consistent with my upbringing and with my belief system. Therefore, as I read Dr. Peale's suggestions and advice for developing a positive mindset, I didn't have to remold any of my basic beliefs.

The ability to think positively is a prerequisite to self-confidence. Make no mistake about this: No matter what business or what profession you are working in, if you don't have a basic belief in yourself, you are not likely to do very well.

The Holy Bible also teaches positive thinking as told by Jesus Christ. One of my favorite passages using the positive principle is found in the parable of the talents (Matthew 25: 14-30). This passage begins: "For the kingdom of heaven is as a man traveling to a far country, who called his own servants and delivered unto them his goods. And unto one he gave five talents, to another two, to another one; to every man according to his several ability; and straightway took his journey."

The Bible says the man gave talents (a monetary unit) to every servant according to each servant's several abilities. Therefore, the man considered the number of talents he should give to each servant based upon what he had observed about each of them. The fact that two of the servants received more than one talent most likely means the man had observed more from the two. Upon the man's return from his journey, the servant that had been given five talents had been true to his character as he had traded and doubled his talents. The servant that had received two talents had also lived true to his character as he had doubled his talents. The servant that had received one talent had also lived true to his character by showing the man that he was right in allocating the fewest number of talents to him. Living up to his low expectations of himself, the servant had buried his one talent, and had not done anything to multiply his gift. The man then took the one talent from the servant that buried it, and gave it to one of his more industrious servants.

I see this passage as a directive to us to use what we have, no matter how much or how little it is, to do more. God wants us to be positive and self-confident with whatever he gives us or allows us to obtain, because it is only through positive thinking that we can multiply what we have. Positive thinking allows us to believe we can do more and accomplish more. We believe this because *we believe* we are capable. By believing this, we actually become capable, and therefore are able to achieve more.

Self-defeating, negative thinking tells us just the opposite. It mocks and scorns us, leading us to believe we are incapable of accomplishing anything. And if we allow this negative thinking to prevail, it will cause us to bury our talents by not making the effort to do more than is absolutely necessary in order to accomplish our daily responsibilities and tasks, or to do our job at work.

In this passage, I believe God is telling us in very clear language that each one of us will be rewarded in life based on our willingness to do what we can to achieve more using what we have.

In black America, many people still believe they can't do more because they are being held back by "The Man" or by "the system." Whether or not this is true is irrelevant, because there is always something a person can do to improve his or her own lot in life. But by repeating this or similar negative statements, a person will begin to believe he or she cannot accomplish certain things. It may be true that our parents, other older relatives, or older friends—long before our time, were actually not able to do certain things based solely on their race. But carrying this antiquated mindset into the 21st Century, whether or not there is any truth to it, can only serve to keep people from realizing all they are capable of accomplishing. Harboring and speaking this negative mindset will only serve to set the groundwork for negative thinking that will surely serve to hinder the positive possibilities of future generations.

No matter who you are, or what racial or ethnic background you identify with, you can break out of that negative-thinking mold. You must nurture and develop a "can-do" spirit and you must allow it to shine and to illuminate all aspects of your life. Your attitude about everything should be positive. You should think positively about your job (no matter how bad it is, if you're still there, there has to be something positive about it). You should think positively about what you are capable of doing (regardless of your education or skill level, quality is free. You can do better at whatever it is that you do).

Even when you go to church, you should think positively. In the church I attend, I'm glad to say my pastor thinks positively. I have visited churches, however, where the message of the sermon seems to leave worshippers with a very negative feeling, sure that there is nothing they can do to keep from going to hell. Sometimes the subtle message given in church leads people to feel that if you have money, or if you have learned to make money, there is something sinister about it which will keep you from going to heaven. It leaves some with the impression that heaven must be reserved for the poor.

But as I understand the Bible, this is not the case. The Bible I study tells me the rich, the poor, and everybody else has an equal chance to go to heaven because the amount of money you have is not necessarily an indication of the kind of person you are in the eyes of God. In other words, material wealth has nothing to do with it. As I understand it, our actions and our belief in God will determine whether or not our soul will get into heaven, not how much or how little money we have in our bank account when we go to our final resting place. Remember, none of us will be taking any material wealth with us, and there will be people from rich, poor, and middle-income backgrounds in heaven and in hell.

## The Attitude Of A Great Salesman

When I was growing up in rural Mississippi, members of my family were farmers. In fact, generations of my ancestors had also been farmers. In some circles in rural Mississippi, people in my family were considered to be pretty sizeable farmers. But in the whole scheme of things, we were really small farmers. However, on our small farm, we grew different crops for different seasons. This allowed us to optimize use of our soil. In the summer, the major crops were cotton and corn. In the spring we would grow peas, beans, and cucumbers. After we picked the cotton, we would plant the peas so that their vines could climb up on the cotton stalks. In the fall we would grow English peas. In the spring of one year, when I was in high school, we had a real bumper crop of string beans. They were back breakers to pick and I hated it with a passion. One evening we spread out the beans that we had gathered so that they would remain fresh. We put them in sacks because we were going to take them to Jackson, Mississippi the next morning. We didn't want the heat to go through them and dry them out. We got up early the next morning and packed up all of the beans, and my father and I got in our truck and headed out to Jackson.

My father had planned to sell all of the beans at the farmer's market. When we got there, every booth that was selling beans had more beans than they needed. Apparently everyone had enjoyed a bumper bean crop. I felt badly because I knew it had been expensive for us to take the beans to Jackson and we had paid other people to help us gather our crop. Now we were stuck with these beans and could not sell them. So when we finished going all the way through the market and couldn't find a buyer, I knew we were going to have to go back home with our beans in tow.

I didn't know what we were going to do. Soon my father said, "Well, I'll tell you what I'm going to do. I'll drive and when I get to one of these grocery stores you go in and tell them that we have fresh green beans, and we are selling them at a good price."

We found out what the grocery stores were paying for their beans from the wholesalers and we set our price just below that. We went to the big supermarkets with names like Jitney Jungle and Piggly Wiggly. (Some of you may not remember these companies but they operated successfully for many years in Mississippi.) The first couple of stores that we went to told us that they had plenty of beans and no matter what the price they were not interested in buying any of ours. At about the fourth or fifth store we went to, the grocer asked, "What is your price?" I told him and he asked if the beans were fresh. I said "yes." He asked if he could see them. I said "sure." We went out to the truck and he saw the beans. They looked fresh and he could tell from looking at them that they were good. My father had sprinkled a little water on some of them to make them look fresh. Finally, the grocer said, "I'll take them all."

Going back home I told my father that I had thought we were going to have to take all the beans back home and that we were not going to make any money on them. He said to me, "Son, there are two things you are going to have to remember in life. The person who is afraid to take a chance on anything will never accomplish anything. And the person who gives up too easily will never make it. I was determined that, if it took all day today and tomorrow, before we went back home we were going to sell all of those beans to somebody. I didn't have any use for them at home, so we were going to sell them to somebody. If you have the ability to take risks and the faith to see it through, the odds are that you will succeed."

## The Attitude of Enthusiasm

Lack of enthusiasm will reduce your chances for success in just about anything. It doesn't matter whether you are getting ready to write a book, work on any kind of project, become part of any kind of team, participate in any type of sport, play a video game, or just a simple game of checkers. It doesn't matter. If you are going to become involved in any activity that requires thought or actions on your part, your enthusiasm (or the lack of it) will determine whether you will succeed or fail. And if you're starting a business, no matter what kind of business it is, the lack of enthusiasm from the people who run the business, who are responsible or in charge of the operation, will reduce its chances of success. Therefore, it is imperative, if you want to accomplish anything of significance, that you have enthusiasm.

Nowhere in life is this principle more apparent than in the area of sales. And if you are in business, make no mistake about it—you are in sales.

I'd like to ask you to use your imagination for a moment. I know some of you won't have to use your imagination to understand what I am about to say, because you have experienced this yourself.

Let's go back to church on Sunday. Let's say your regular pastor isn't there, but there is a pastor standing there in the pulpit, preaching. You stand there in the isle, and you listen to him to for a moment. What is he doing? He is trying to sell the gospel to the congregation. And you know he is selling a product that is strong because it has stood for centuries. It has been "sold" for centuries. Now, the gospel according to Jesus Christ has to be strong if it has come through hundreds—and now thousands—of years. Since I'm a firm believer in this gospel, I know for a fact that it is indeed strong.

Thinking of the gospel of Jesus Christ as a product, let's look at something for a moment. Even when you are selling a product that is proven to work and that has been a strong, best-selling product for centuries, if you listen to someone standing there talking about it in a monotone voice, as if it is a *big burden* to sell, you are not going to like it; nor is it going to penetrate the unbeliever. In fact, it may appear to the unbeliever that the preacher has not accepted Christ, or that if he has, it has not set him on fire.

The same thing is true when you are selling anything else. Why would somebody buy from you when *you* appear not to believe in what you're selling?

No matter what product you are trying to sell, if you cannot get excited about it and have enthusiasm about it, you need to stop selling that product. Go find something else or get out of the business. Find a product that you can be passionate about.

I know about selling real estate. I also know that anyone selling real estate should have a lot of enthusiasm about helping someone purchase a home. Why? First of all, I know that a home is one of the three basic essentials of life, included among food, clothing and shelter. I also know that while in some places on earth, people can use trees or bushes for shelter, in America, we want to live in apartments and houses, whether they are rented or owned. I also know most people want to realize the American dream of home ownership, and that when you sell real estate you are helping them secure the American dream as well as providing them with one of life's essentials—shelter.

The Century 21 Galloway-Herron mission is: To sell real estate knowing you're providing what is most likely the greatest investment a person will make. "Our mission is to improve the quality of life for our clients, customers and agents by providing the finest real estate financial services the world has ever known, and—in the process, to create raving fans while having fun."

Most Americans who reach age 65 really have a small net worth, or no financial net worth at all. Those who have net worth in excess of $50,000, with the exception of two or three percent, have the bulk of their wealth invested in their home. So when you're selling real estate, you are selling one of the best investments that have withstood the test of time, and will continue to stand—as one of America's best investment options.

When you sell real estate, you're also selling a tax advantage. You can deduct the interest paid and the taxes paid on a home. This helps to decrease the total amount of taxes that have to be paid on April 15th of each year.

When you sell real estate, you're also selling personal pride and self-esteem. Because owning a home says something good about a person; it makes a positive statement. It says you have done something fantastic that millions of people have not been able to do. It says you now stand among the "haves" instead of among the "have-nots." And, home ownership gives you "clout" at the bank. It is a fact that when a person who owns a home goes to apply for credit for other things, whether to go into business or just to buy a piece of land, the fact that he or she owns a home is going to increase his or her chance of getting the needed credit to be able to do these things.

In short, when you are a real estate agent, when all's said and done, you are selling happiness and joy. You're helping a person or families acquire something that is most likely going to be one of their most prized possessions. And as an agent you're also fixing that person's or that family's cost of living expenses to a certain degree. So you're helping them to manage their finances as well. If the homebuyer has a fixed rate mortgage, the only related expenses that will rise are the taxes and the insurance. And one day, the mortgage will be paid off and all the buyer will have to pay are taxes and insurance. So as a real estate agent, you are one of the factors standing between someone having a comfortable and secure place to live after retirement, or not.

When you are a real estate agent, and you help someone purchase a home, you are saving them from paying the high and ever-increasing cost of renting from month to month. When a person is renting a home instead of buying it, as the owner's property taxes and insurance increase, and the cost of other things go up along with inflation in general, the renter is going to have to pay more rent from year to year.

Therefore, if you're a real estate agent and you don't sell a person a home, you're helping to ensure that as a renter, they'll end up paying more rent when they retire than they are paying while they're younger and still able to work. Generally when people retire their income is less than when they are working. So you end up with a higher cost of living after you retire (a time of life when you need it to be lower). But just the reverse happens when a person is buying a home as opposed to renting. The homebuyer ends up having a lower housing expense after retirement.

So, a real estate sales agent needs to sell his or her product as enthusiastically as possible, because this product is going to help determine the financial outcome of someone's life. And as someone who genuinely cares about the well being of others, it is the real estate agent's duty (and his or her responsibility) to do everything within their power to help a person find a way to purchase a home.

If you are interested in being a top salesperson in real estate or in any other kind of business or endeavor, you should reread and understand the information I'm discussing in this section on enthusiasm. You should read the subtle messages as well as the overt ones, because they're all written to help you succeed in sales, and in life. Enthusiasm is crucial for any salesperson—make no mistake about it, we are all salespeople. No matter what you are doing or what you are selling, you will become better at doing it or at selling it if you learn to add a hefty dose of enthusiasm to it.

As far as I am concerned, your courage, your confidence, and all of your soul's intensity is demonstrated when you show enthusiasm.

Here's a case in point. I was walking the streets of Los Angeles alone one night. I had taken the bus to where I was going. When I got off the bus as I was returning home, I was headed toward my apartment and I saw this tough-looking guy coming towards me on the opposite side of the street. I felt really frightened because it was very late at night and I didn't want or need any trouble. I thought quickly to myself, "This guy is going to be less likely to mess with me if he thinks I am as tough as he is." So I gathered together my enthusiasm and confidently strode across the pavement, and got on the same side of the street he was on. I boldly started walking straight toward him. When I walked past him, I saw he was afraid of me because he stopped, moved to the side, and watched me as I walked right past him and kept on my way. I learned that night that sometimes, if you show a little courage even when you are really frightened, you can, with confidence and enthusiasm, drive danger from your path.

## The Link Between Health and Attitude

I am no health expert. But what I do know is that the better I feel, the more productive I become. I know that when I feel badly or think badly about myself I am less productive. I know that when I am dressed in a suit that I'm proud of, and that I feel good wearing, I have more power to achieve my goals. I know that when I feel better, I have much more power to accomplish what I'm trying to do.

For many years, every morning, Monday thru Friday, my wife and I hit the street and walked two miles at a brisk pace. Now, we go upstairs to our exercise room in our home. I do this for two reasons. First of all, I want to be in good physical condition and I am determined not to be overweight. They tell me that your chances of medical problems increase in proportion to the more you weigh in excess of what you ought to weigh. When it comes to weight, I believe medical doctors know what they are talking about.

From my personal experience, I feel like doing more when I feel sharp and look sharp. Dr. Kent Cooper, who has become a legend here in Dallas, has the Aerobics Center and has written a lot material about good health and exercise. I believe Dr. Cooper knows what he is talking about. I've seen him on TV and I've listened to him on radio talk shows as he has discussed how you can lessen your chances of a heart attack when you spend the time to keep yourself in shape.

The other part of keeping yourself in good physical condition has to do with what you eat. Historically, my family ate a lot of fried foods, pork, beef, and—of course—fish and chicken. But we always had more than a healthy dose of pork and beef. Again, I believe the experts when they warn us to stay away from excessive amounts of fried foods. I believe they're right in telling us to eat more chicken, fish, and baked foods. In my family we are doing this. We are paying attention to what we believe we can do for ourselves to help us live a long and healthy life. There is plenty of expert advice on the market today about food and diet, and its effects on your health. And if you're interested in improving your health or in losing weight, you can pick and choose an eating plan that works best for you. But I am convinced that for any of us to operate more effectively and efficiently, our health has to be good.

Once when my mother-in-law was sick, doctors told her she needed surgery. So we took her to the doctor in the small town where she lived. The doctor walked in and it appeared that he needed help to get around because he was so fat that he was out of breath just from walking into the room. He exhibited a great lack of enthusiasm for his work, and he seemed to be in very poor health himself. He made us feel that there was no hope of curing my mother-in-law. After talking with him we decided we needed to go somewhere else to see another doctor.

As soon as we walked out of the door of his office, my wife Lela said, "Let's not go back to this man again." Later I found out that in the community, many people referred to this doctor as "Dr. Death," because most of his patients that were really ill always died. I believe part of the reason this happened is because that doctor did not have enthusiasm for the practice of medicine. He did not seem to believe in himself, and he did not believe his patients could live. And since the doctor didn't believe they could live, the patients didn't believe they could live either. So they died.

I am asking you, right here, and right now, to look for and find it within yourself to love yourself more. When you do, you will begin to feel more enthusiastic about your job, and about how you do your job every day. You will become a poster child for enthusiasm. You'll want to look good, you'll want to feel good, and you will be better able to begin achieving whatever it is you are trying to accomplish in your life.

## *Summary of Step 3*
## Develop A Positive Attitude

IN A NUTSHELL: Develop a positive attitude about work. Learn to be enthusiastic. Learn to "sell" yourself and your skills and services expertly, every day, at the job you have now. Become enthusiastic about yourself, your health, your family, your life, your job, and your future. Do this, and you'll be helping to set the stage for increased earning power on your way to becoming a millionaire.

*Step 4*

# Control Your Expenses

4

I once attended a seminar at which the speaker asked a group of 100 people if they were saving money monthly. At least half of them said they *were saving*.

His next question was whether they were making more money today than they were making three years ago. Every hand in the room was raised.

Then he asked who was saving more money today than they were saving three years ago. Only two hands were raised.

He finally asked how many in the audience were in worst financial condition than they were in three years earlier. It appeared that at least ninety percent raised their hands.

The point he was making is, no matter how much money we earn, we still spend more—proportionately. Granted, as people move up the income ladder, they also move up even higher on the expense side. Still, the man was saying it is crucial to keep expenditures under control by not purchasing anything you cannot pay for (afford), or that will put you outside the formula you set up in Step 2 to use for your savings and expenditures.

What this speaker was saying rings truer today than ever. We live in a time where people want to live lavishly like the rich people they see on television shows and in advertisements, and that they read about in magazines displaying the extravagant lifestyles of the rich and famous.

In doing their best to mimic such people, or to appear to be successful when they may not be, too many people are purchasing expensive things, such as luxury automobiles, before they are actually in a position to do so. But listen to this: Any man or woman who buys a Cadillac, a Mercedes, or any other kind of expensive car—before he or she owns a home—has mixed up priorities. In fact, a person who spends in this way has a "poverty mentality."

When it comes to automobiles, a family should have what is necessary to take them to work and to other places they must go. In other words, they need basic transportation only. Those people who believe the car makes the person are falsely equating a big, "fine" car with success and prosperity. But that is not true prosperity, and only people who have less knowledge of financial matters than you will be impressed by idiotic indulgences. While it is true that a luxury car has the appearance of wealth, it is not actually wealth when measured as an appreciable asset. Automobiles are expense items. They require maintenance and they depreciate rapidly; therefore, they are a drain on wealth. Consequently, a person with an automobile with costs above his means is working against himself by making an expensive "vanity" statement that ultimately reduces his quality of life.

*As* a rule of thumb, you should *control your expenses* in such a way that you always have money reserved for savings and investments. This chapter is like most of the information presented in this book. It is not new. But it is a mystery to many—if not most, people. Therefore, I am doing my best to present this information in a way that will get your attention, because there is truly nothing spectacular about what this book is teaching.

I want you to believe you can become a millionaire. I know this might seem hard to believe, especially when you have been raised in a family of meager means, and when you might still be facing hard financial times, and all around you are people who are either in poverty, poor, or working hard just to make ends meet. I realize it might be hard indeed for you to believe you can actually become a millionaire. It might be hard for you to "see yourself" becoming a millionaire, but that is exactly what you must do. In order to do it, however, you are going to need a paradigm shift. You are going to have to change the way you see your life and your potential. I am offering you a blueprint to follow in order to accomplish your paradigm shift. Now, if you will do what I am telling you to do, you will be following an example that has helped me achieve what you wish to achieve. Of course, you millionaires, just say "Amen."

In the remainder of this brief chapter, I am going to offer you some ways to control your expenses. Just remember that when you spend all your money, you are living just to help the rich to become even richer. On the other hand, if you keep all your money and save it, you are not allowing your money to do all it can do for you. You need to have a talk with the person you see in the mirror and make him or her understand that you need to use some of that money to make more money. In addition, if you implement the suggestions in this book, I know you will find yourself with more money left over every month for saving, and you will be able to see and feel your purse or wallet getting fatter.

## Whenever Possible, Spend Cash

During the Christmas holiday about 15 years ago I was standing in line to pay, after shopping for a gift for my wife, Lela. The man just before me in line pulled cash out of his pocket to pay his bill. We had been talking for some time, so he turned to me and said, "I pay in cash." I told him I do that as well, only I use checks. He said, "No, that is not cash. That's not what I'm talking about. You see this cash I'm holding? This is what I am talking about."

My question to him was, "What's the big deal? I am not using a credit card, and the store takes my check just as though it is cash." The man said, "That may be true, but I am not using cash for the benefit of the store. My wife and I have discovered that when we pay with cash—using money—we don't spend as much, especially my wife. It's far easier to pay out money when you use checks, and too easy when you use credit cards."

One day I mentioned to my lawyer, Bill Mayhomes, about what this man had said to me about spending less when using cash money. He responded that he could not see how it would make any difference with me because from his observation I did not want to spend money in any form and he could not imagine how I could spend less unless I wanted to starve my wife and children. He said the only reason I am confident that you are not doing that is I saw Lela and the children and they look to be in excellent condition. Also, I know Lela and she would not allow it to happen.

Every time I think about getting rid of that lawyer, I think better of it, concluding that a good lawyer is one who does not just tell you what you want to hear.

Getting back to the point, you will spend less money if you spend actual cash money, as opposed to using checks or credit cards. It's psychological. When you can actually see your money—your real money—disappearing, you get a better mental picture of your bank account being emptied.

Be careful with cash, because it can be a magnet for robbers and thieves. So I would never recommend that you carry around large amounts of money, announcing to the world that you carry cash. But whenever possible, give yourself a mental splash of cold water, by paying in cash. It might help bring back a needed dose of "realism" to your spending habits.

## Control Spending on Bad Habits

Be aware of the personal and financial costs of your habits. Spending on bad habits can be the kiss of death to your plan of becoming a millionaire. Any money spent on buying drugs (unless prescribed by a reputable physician) or alcohol can cause problems with your financial planning. The biggest problem occurs not just because of the extra money you're spending on these things. The biggest problem comes when your drug or drinking problems get control of you. The influence of these substances can obscure your thinking and judgment, and you cannot see that you are out of control. Of course, you will eventually have legal problems and health problems, all of which will cause you to have to spend even more money. Besides draining your bank account, your bad habits might even put you in a position where you must miss work, or you might perform poorly at work, thereby reducing your income. Or they could eliminate your income altogether by getting you fired from your job.

Bad habits will catch up with you, and they will eventually take you under if you don't find a way to regain control of yourself.

Here's a case in point. I received a call one day from a client we had sold a house to more than 20 years earlier. He said he needed to come by and talk with me about his financial situation. He related that he was about to lose his home. I assumed he had purchased a new home, since he had owned the one my company helped him purchase for 20 years or more. So I set an appointment for him to come talk to me.

The man came in and told me he had 23 credit cards. He said he was in debt for over $67,000 with these cards. I kept asking him why he had accumulated so much credit-card debt. He hemmed and hawed a while, and finally said "overspending" is what had caused this problem. From my observation and from what I knew about this family, I knew the excessive spending was not on cars, clothes, jewelry, or any of those kinds of things. So I suggested that maybe he could use his home to get a home equity loan. He told me he had already taken out a home equity loan. That's when I began to realize there had to be something going on I was not being told about. So I told him I would not be able to help him unless he talked to me about the real problem that was causing all the spending. He took a long, deep breath and then he finally said, "Well, I'll tell you. It's gambling." I then asked him what kind of gambling he was involved in. He said, "Going to the boat."

People in Dallas and surrounding areas understand this phrase to mean going to Shreveport, Louisiana, to the casinos. My recommendation to this man was that he should seek professional help for his gambling problem first (even the casinos advertise a help line for people who have lost control). I felt sure that if he got his gambling problem under control, he would surely find a way to solve his financial problems.

I try not to think too badly about people with problems caused by indulging in bad habits. You see I realize that—but for the grace of God, it could be you or me in that predicament. I have been blessed by God to have had the parents and the upbringing I had, so I know I should not look down upon people who don't have the will or the desire to resist temptations such as gambling, or the lure to "get rich quick." This man had allowed his desire for "fast, easy money" to outweigh his common sense about money and finance. Years ago when we sold him his home, he clearly had the financial understanding and wherewithal to purchase a home. But some time after purchasing the home, he lost touch with that part of his conscience that had to be screaming to him to stop, as he was losing control of his finances to his gambling addiction.

Bad habits are like that. That's why we call them "bad habits." They are bad for us, and they eventually cause us more problems than we can solve. Bad habits can look good on the outside. They can appear to offer a lot of fun, and many of them are certainly presented to us in glamorous and fun-filled packages. But if we are not careful, indulging in something that looks like fun, habitually, can become a problem that will derail financial stability.

## Plan and Save for Large Expenses

Lela and I have never had more than one car payment at a time. Since we've been married, we have always owned two or three cars, but we have never had more than one car payment at a time. How have we done this? We made the decision early in our married life that we could not afford to make two car payments and a house payment at the same time. We purposely kept our payments low enough where one paycheck could take care of our living expenses, just in case one of us could not work.

Every time we purchase a new automobile, the last one we bought has to be paid in full. We also keep our cars from 10 to 12 years before buying another one. The average family keeps a car from 3 to 5 years. Therefore, most people always have at least one car payment. That means as soon as they get their car paid for, they feel they need a new car, and it often comes with even higher monthly payments than the last one.

But when you keep your car for at least three years after paying for it, you get a chance to save some of the money that you would normally be spending on a car note. For example, if your note is $600 a month, you can save $7,200 per year, and $27,600 in three years. That is money that can get your savings program well underway, enabling you to begin investing money in a way that can bring you real wealth.

Sure, having an older automobile means your car will get out of warranty, and it may cost you more to maintain than a new car would cost. However, it will not cost $7,200 per year to maintain a car that is out of warranty. You can also purchase an extended warranty, as we do, to help you maintain an older car.

If your older car is in really bad repair, you can consider purchasing a used car, or a demonstrator. As you know, when you purchase a new car, the day you drive from the car lot you have a significant loss of value in depreciation. But when you purchase a car with a few thousand miles on it, someone else has already taken the "depreciation hit." That means you are lowering your overall costs when you purchase a used vehicle as opposed to a brand new one. Saving $3,600 on a purchase can save you in excess of $100 per month when you include the interest payment on an auto loan for a brand new car.

Taking inventory of the condition of your automobile is something you should do periodically. You need to be sure you actually need a new car before you purchase one. If you are the type of person who has to "keep up with the Joneses," and you feel you have to buy a new car so that you're not the only one on the block without a fine, shiny new car, then you may not have the mindset for acquiring real wealth. You may be too wrapped up, tied-up, and tangled-up in being among the "trendy" crowd. That kind of thinking and that kind of lifestyle costs money, and it can rob you of financial stability as well.

## Control the Cost of Credit

Some of you love getting those shiny new credit cards in the mail. The ability to charge now and pay later is certainly something we all cherish, and it can be a real convenience to own credit cards. But no matter how nice they are to have around, credit card costs can be horrendous when you pay only the minimum every month. On most cards, when you are late making your payment, you are charged a large fee, such as $29 or $39 over the amount of the payment that is due.

At one time in my life, I had a card from a major bank. Even though I paid the total amount due one month, they still charged me a small amount of interest on the money that I still owed, because I did not pay the balance in full. The balance was not more than $15, and the next month I failed to pay even that amount on time. Then I was charged with a $29 late fee.

Let me urge you to remember that late fees are avoidable, and so is enormous credit-card debt. Get rid of a pocket full of cards and streamline your credit opportunities. Put the credit card companies on a "welfare" program using a "Reverse Robin Hood" program.

Credit-card cost is something you can control. You must arrange to pay your debt by the due date each month, and not allow them to build up late fees. Remember, this information is kept in your credit bureau files, so you are lowering your credit score every time you allow these due dates to pass by with your bills unpaid.

How many credit cards does a person need? I know of a family that once had 27 credit cards with a combined balance of $137,000. And this is not a joke; they were actually too broke to go bankrupt. How can this be? They could not find a way to pay the attorney to take their bankruptcy case, and they did not have the money to pay the filing fee. Therefore, they could not afford to file for bankruptcy. Yes, they were TOO BROKE TO GO BANKRUPT.

Therefore, be alert when it comes to credit cards and credit-card debt. It can take years to plow from under the burden of heavy credit-card debt. Watch out for those cards that not only charge an exorbitant amount of money in late fees, but that take your interest rate to as high as 25% and over. They sometimes get you to take out a new card with the promise of a low interest rate, or in some cases no interest, for a certain time period. But this offer or provision is good only if you are not late paying your bill, or if you do not go over your spending limit.

The bottom line is you have to read the fine print when credit-card offers seem too good to be true. There is usually a "catch," and if you are not paying attention, more and more of your hard-earned money will get caught up in the catch.

## *Summary of Step 4*
## Control Your Expenses

Yes, you can learn to control your expenses. Just as you can learn to develop a habit of saving money, you can also learn to watch with great care how you spend it. I'm not telling you to become a modern-day Ebenezer Scrooge, but I am saying you should not act as though every day is Christmas. You have to introduce discipline into your spending routine, if you expect to become a millionaire using my plan. It simply will not work with out-of-control spending habits. So learn to control your spending, you'll be taking a giant step towards using your income from your job to make you a millionaire.

*Step 5*

# How to Establish Good Credit, Improve Bad Credit

5 The next step on the road to becoming a millionaire is the establishment of good credit. Some people might consider "credit" to be a "four-letter word," but it is actually something you should learn to treasure. It shouldn't frighten you or send chills down your spine. Credit is good. But how you handle your credit can be good or bad.

## Make Good Credit a Habit

The best way to have good credit is to make it a habit and a practice to pay your bills in a timely manner. If it is already too late for you to begin doing this "early in life," then you must begin to do it now.

America still runs on credit. The government operates on credit, and so does everything else. And while individual citizens can get credit, unfortunately, we can't do like the American government, and go raise our debt ceiling every year so that we can just keep going deeper and deeper into debt, with taxpayers footing the bill.

Since we can't do this, we really have to guard our credit.

Why is credit important? Weren't you listening? I just said that America runs on credit. Living in a country that runs on credit means credit is going to be important to and for everyone. So, since personal credit is so important to and for America and Americans, for a moment, let's look at credit and the individual.

With very few exceptions, the first credit many of us Americans get is the result of getting a credit card or buying a car. Although it doesn't take impeccable credit to buy a car, you must have some credit. This means car credit is fairly easy to get.

A lot of us like to travel, to see America (and the world). If you're among this set, you need to own the major credit cards: American Express, Visa, Master Card, Discover and others. To obtain these cards requires fairly good credit, and getting some of them requires having a better credit rating than others. Today, a lot of companies have eased their requirements, and almost anyone can have some kind of card, some with higher interest rates.

Good credit is essential to living "the American Dream." Because when Americans finally get tired of the landlord raising their rent, as millions of Americans have done, they begin to look into home ownership. And guess what? Unless you're rich enough to pay cash for a home, it takes good credit to get a mortgage with a good interest rate.

So now I know you're starting to see clearly why credit is so important to living in America—the country that runs on credit.

Now if you're an individual who happens to have inherited millions of dollars from a rich relative, maybe credit is not so important to you. But wait. Even rich people use credit! Why? Because it's easier (and most often safer) to use than cash. Using credit cards allows you to keep automatic records of expenses, making it easier to see where your money is going. Credit card statements offer a monthly picture of your spending habits revealing your lifestyle—along with your good and/or bad spending habits. Smart people who understand credit, and who want to protect theirs, will use this information to make any necessary spending adjustments.

When it comes to credit, it should be clear that if you're going to participate in "the good life" in America, embracing the whole American dream (and that includes homeownership, the purchase of large consumer items like automobiles, and going into business for yourself), then you've got to have credit to be able to borrow the money you need to have to do what you will need to do.

Therefore, it is necessary to fully understand and appreciate why you need credit, and for each of us to realize how important it is to have good credit. The logical thing to start talking about is how to get credit and how to keep it good. I think the way to do that is to first talk about what *not* to do if you intend to have good credit.

Sometimes, people have already experienced a little credit when first leaving their parents' home. Basically, when you come out of high school, you don't have any credit history. This is the perfect time to begin establishing good habits concerning the use of credit so you will be able to enter the market with good credit. Your parents may have helped you establish your first form of credit. If your mother or father has set you up with a credit card, or co-signed on a consumer loan with you, you need to make timely payments and take the loan or credit privilege seriously. You need to keep it current, and treat it like it is something precious and important to you.

If you have a student loan, don't ever allow that loan to go into default and have judgments against you. That will go into your credit file, and it's absolutely unnecessary. If you are ever not able to repay your loan, you can apply for economic hardship forbearance, or a deferment. (Go to your student loan company's web site to find out more about these things.)

What I am saying is you should not allow your credit to become bad, or to go into default. You must remember that credit is a privilege that can be denied if it is abused. If it is denied, it will certainly obstruct your options or will not allow you to choose the different paths in life that you may want to choose. Your credit can hinder you from such things as going into business, buying a home, buying an automobile, or doing other kinds of things that you can do if you have good credit. In fact, your credit history could even keep you from getting the job you want.

For someone with absolutely no credit, the simplest thing to do—and the fastest way to get credit going without having people co-sign for you—is to go to the bank and borrow some money. For example, you could borrow $1,000. After borrowing it, leave the money in the bank as collateral, and pay off the loan on a monthly basis. Agree that you're going to repay it in one year, or two years, etc. Then, pay it off in that time, or ahead of time, so that you can begin to establish good credit. It may be good to pay it off, and then, borrow again. That starts your credit history.

The reason that you can get the $1,000 from the bank, even if you do not have an established record with the bank, is that you are now establishing your credit record with that bank. The money that you borrow is not going to leave the bank and remains there as collateral for the loan. The bank is taking no risks. When you pay off the debt, then you have $1,000 free and clear in the bank. The banks will do this.

## A Way to Improve Bad Credit

This same strategy can be used to improve bad credit. Instead of just being able to go to the bank and get a loan, however, you will probably have to get a secured loan. To do this, you'll need to have in a savings account the same amount of money you will be asking the bank to lend you, and you'll use the savings account you set up for this purpose as collateral. Then, once you repay the loan (and try to pay it off early), you will have established some good credit that can offset some not-so-good information in your credit file.

I think the point I just made is one that should come as a welcome surprise to a lot of people with less-than-perfect credit. The fact that you can have some bad credit information in your file, along with some very good credit information, means you can re-build your credit history. You can show potential lenders that even though you might have gone through rough periods in the past where your credit suffered, that you have now changed your lifestyle and payment habits to reflect the credit profile you desire to have for your future.

It used to be that one of the easiest forms of credit to obtain was a gasoline card. I remember that when I was in college, companies mailed me applications for these cards before I graduated. Today, college students get inundated with too many offers for credit cards, and, unfortunately, too many students are taking these companies up on these offers at a time when they need to be turning them down.

Let me urge you to be <u>deliberate</u> about building or re-building good credit. Get a gasoline credit card or some other type of card that is fairly easy to obtain. Then, be sure to pay the card-issuing companies on a timely basis on or before the payments are due. Now you are started on your way to having good credit.

Initially, until people are able to establish a certain amount of control over what they are doing in their financial affairs, they don't really need anything other than a gas card, and one major credit card such as American Express, Master Card or Visa. One of these cards will allow you to buy almost anything. Any of these, plus a major department store credit card is actually a lot of credit.

Let me warn you, if you're new to credit, to be careful not to fall into the trap caused by having good credit. Let me explain. The minute you get one card and meet your financial obligations with it, this will cause you to qualify to get all the cards in the world. Since this is true, a person who doesn't have control over their spending can easily wind up in "good credit"-card trouble, because it's easy to spend yourself into out-of-control debt when the cards are easy to obtain.

When I got out of school, I had a couple of major gas cards. Then, I got the American Express and a Sears card. And that's what we stayed with for a long time.

Now, what if a person says, "Well, I didn't know all this about credit before reading this book. I've already made a lot of the mistakes this book could have saved me from making. Had I known all these before, I would have done things differently, and I would have kept my credit record clean. Now, I already have a bad credit claim on my record."

My comment to this person would still be the same: Proceed to borrow the money as I said, set up that bank credit, and pay back the loan. But remember, this time you know it's serious business, and you know you cannot falter. You are being given another chance, but you have to do your part. So do it. Go ahead and establish some good credit.

## What Good Credit Really Means

I've referred to good and bad credit and it may not be obvious to some people what good credit actually is. Good credit is where you have established debt with a lender. Maybe it is through use of a credit card, a department store card, a mortgage or an unsecured loan at a bank.

What is important in credit is that you owe somebody (or a group of parties), and you have a responsibility to pay on a monthly basis or over some other specified period of time. When you apply for new credit, or nowadays when you apply for some jobs and even some auto insurance, the credit reporting bureaus gives information about your credit history to other credit or lending organizations. And good credit would be referred to as your history of having paid all your creditors on a timely basis every month as you agreed to do when you established your credit.

Your credit starts to be referred to as "not good," "fair," or even or even "poor," when there is evidence that you've been slow paying—or paying more than 30 to 60 days late. That is referred to in credit-bureau language as "slow pay." Having "bad credit" means some lender has pursued you for payment on a particular obligation for which you didn't pay, and they placed a judgment against you, or they charged off the loan made to you against their profit and loss statement. Judgments and "charge-offs" are items referred to as bad pieces of credit. A combination of these items on your credit report will get you into the bad credit situation.

First of all, if a person has not had any judgments, but has been paying extremely slowly, it is fairly easy to correct the credit. All he or she has to do is to begin to pay people on time. It's a self-correcting situation. It's a simple matter and in time, his or her credit will be cured. If you've found yourself in any of these "slow pay" situations, you should immediately start paying those accounts on time.

If you have had a charge-off, or repossession, it will take years under normal circumstances before that comes off your record. Still, even though this is true, today many lenders and businesses are willing to take a chance on people with less than optimal credit history. Usually, however, anything you purchase under these "special" circumstances may come with unusually high interest rates.

People who have slow payments and judgments should start paying on time on those items that are now "slow," and they should try to make arrangements with creditors on the judgments. Many times you can pay and get judgments settled for 50 cents on the dollar or 25 cents on the dollar. It's quite possible that a $1,000 judgment could be settled for $250 or less. Even though it will show on your credit record, it will show a zero balance. And having a zero balance show in your credit file is better than having a judgment in it. In addition, you can sometimes get your creditors to write a letter that you can send to the major credit reporting bureaus showing the judgment was resolved in a satisfactory way.

There is no blanket way to handle all credit problems, and I'm no expert on correcting credit. There are all kinds of credit counselors you can go to these days to get good advice about repairing bad credit. If you seek out this kind of advice, be sure you are dealing with a reputable company, and that you don't get caught up in some kind of scheme promising to "erase" bad credit. In fact, it might be a good idea to check with the Better Business Bureau to see if they have a file on a company promising to help you repair your credit. It's better to be safe than sorry.

As I said before, I'm no expert on repairing credit. I'm just speaking from a practical standpoint, based on what I've seen others do, and from my experience in helping people get financing for homes.

One important factor we've noticed in the real estate business is that there are a number of people who have bad credit because they were waiting for someone else to take care of a debt. Often, the first thing people will tell us is, "My insurance company was supposed to pay that hospital bill."

Or they'll say, "That car was a lemon, and I just gave it back." But to the bank or lender, the fact that it was a lemon is unimportant. It has absolutely no meaning. Granted you may be telling the truth, but so many people won't be telling the truth when they say it was a lemon. So lenders typically deal only with promissory notes and the terms and conditions established in granting the credit in the first place. If you buy a car and later discover it has a major problem, you should continue to pay the monthly payments until you get the problem worked out. You should try to get the dealer to fix the car, sell you another car, trade it, or whatever. You should continue making those monthly payments as you committed to do when you arranged for the credit to buy the car. To stop making payments in protest will only hurt your credit rating and future buying power. Remember, you owe the bank, not the dealer.

When it comes to financing automobiles, the money you borrow and the automobile, in most instances, don't come from the same place. So the business that sold you that lemon is not usually the one you're making your car payment to. Generally car loans are financed by banks, savings and loans institutions, credit unions, or in many cases General Motors Acceptance Corporation, Ford Motor Credit Corporation, the Chrysler Corporation, or some other consumer credit organizations.

Although the dealer sold you the car, the money used to pay for it came from a finance company. And even though you did business with both, they are not the same. We sometimes confuse the lender with the seller, when they are seldom the same entity. They could be the same in some instances, i.e., Sears or some other similar enterprise; however, you still deal separately with the merchant and credit-granting side of the business.

When the creditor and the seller of the goods are one and the same, generally, you will not have any problems that cannot be resolved. Even with the automobile dealer, even though it may take a lot of time and patience on your part, and loads of persistence, if you don't give up, you will get just about any problem corrected.

If at all possible, you should avoid letting situations get to the point of repossession. Even if you bought a $2,000 television set that consistently had problems, with good credit you can at least buy another quality product while you pursue your rights under state and federal laws.

As for those who are contemplating filing bankruptcy, I have to tell you I think filings for bankruptcy have just gone crazy. The bankruptcy law is a good law in and of itself. It allows a person who is overextended to get out of that situation. But—in droves—people are making a racket of it. As far as I'm concerned, too many lawyers are just looking for a client when they advise filing for bankruptcy. Far too many people are doing it.

When so-called "big shots" file bankruptcy, many times some of them are not bankrupt at all. They have other resources. For the average working person, bankruptcy is the last resort. No one should want to file bankruptcy, because it will follow you around in your credit file for a very long time. When you try to finance a house or borrow from a bank, a prior bankruptcy will keep you from getting what you want for a period of time. Think of bankruptcy as the absolute last thing you should consider, because when you file for it, you are essentially delaying or perhaps putting off doing some or many of the things you want to do in life.

The same thing applies to the person in business. If there's any way out of a financial bind, other than filing bankruptcy, you should take that route. If you can somehow satisfy your creditors, do that instead.

I have invested in deals and borrowed money on deals that went sour. In fact, for many years I paid back money on a deal that turned sour. So,

I'm urging you based on my own experiences to pay your creditors even when deals have gone sour.

I challenge anybody to tell me what you can get in the business world (unless you have a whole lot of cash on hand) that is of any financial significance, without credit. I'm afraid the truth is: Nothing. Therefore, I know it is far better for you—if it is at all within your means—to pay your creditors.

I also look at it as a moral proposition, and I'm not trying to be holier than thou. Still, I think if you get some money or goods from someone and you promise to pay your debt, you're supposed to pay it. Now I do realize there are certain circumstances where you simply cannot pay, and that's what the bankruptcy law is for.

The law as it relates to bankruptcy changed in 2004. It changed to make it harder for the average consumer to have debts forgiven. The large banks and other credit grantors have teamed up with the current political powers to prevent you from getting that "fresh start" that you could get prior to these changes. At the same time, these changes were made to make it harder for you to get your debts discharged through bankruptcy; it has become easier for you to get more debt. It appears that no matter how low your credit score is, you can probably still get credit under some condition and at some interest rate. If you have a credit score that is in excess of 640, you will most likely be able to purchase a home at the prevailing interest rate. As credit scores fall below 640, into the 500-range or below, you will most likely pay a much higher rate of interest. When credit scores exceed 640, going into the 700-range and above, credit alternatives increase, and no down payment offers become available.

## Path to the "American Dream"

Now, back to the point from which we started.

Very few Americans are going to live and work, and not strive to achieve the American dream. When I say American dream, I'm talking basically about two kinds of things. Being partial to the real estate business, I think home ownership is the ultimate American dream. And being a businessman, I'm convinced that going into business for oneself is also part of the American dream. And I know you're not going to be able to experience either of these aspects of the American dream without good credit.

For the sake of example, let's say you have built up your basic credit, and you've been working for a few years, and now you want to extend your credit to make a large investment or to start a business. In order to do this, you must understand how to establish a credit line at the bank. If you have maintained your good credit, this will just be an extension of what you have already accomplished. Instead of needing a few thousand dollars, you may need tens of thousands, or maybe even hundreds of thousands of dollars. To obtain these types of funds, you will need to utilize a more sophisticated and advanced stage of credit. First you will prepare a financial statement, which is called a "balance sheet." The balance sheet lists all of your assets and debts. Then you subtract the debts from the assets, and that gives you your net worth.

## Personal Balance Sheet

John Q. Jones
Balance Sheet or Financial Statement
June 30, 2005

| ASSETS | |
|---|---|
| Cash | $125,000 |
| Marketable Securities | $10,000 |
| 401k Retirement Plan | $21,000 |
| Automobile | $18,000 |
| Home | $152,000 |
| Household Goods | $27,000 |
| **Total Assets** | **$353,000** |
| **LIABILITIES** | |
| Mortgage Loan | 54,000 |
| Credit Cards | $2,100 |
| Car Loans | $5,200 |
| Miscellaneous Liabilities | $1,800 |
| **Total Liabilities** | **$63,100** |
| **NET WORTH** | **$289,900** |
| **TOTAL LIABILITIES AND NET WORTH** | **$353,000** |

I know that there are cases where a person's debt may be bigger than their assets. If that is the case for you, you're in trouble, because you have what is known as a negative net worth. You are not likely going to get a credit line in this situation. But a banker will lend you money if you have good credit and a source of income that justifies additional credit, whether it's income from your business, or from a job where you have income sufficient to retire a particular debt.

You may have to consider placing personal resources up against the debt. For example, there are some who might have $50,000 in General Motors stock, Sears stock, or equity in real estate. If you're one of these fortunate people, you can put that up as collateral in order to get the $50,000, $75,000, or $100,000 line of credit that you need.

Let's just use for example $100,000. When you apply for a line of credit this large, you will have to put up the necessary resources. You might have to use your financial statement in total. You can go into a lending institution with a financial statement, and just put up the whole statement to get certain amounts of credit. It depends on the requirements of the particular bank.

But the beautiful part about this line of credit is that the day you go in wanting a $100,000 line of credit, and it's actually granted, well, that day you may need only $10,000. That means you now have $90,000 more available to you anytime that you need it.

Typically, the loan will be granted for a specific period of time such as one or two years. The lender will expect you to pay down your debt, at some point, and you always have to service the debt. Servicing the debt is the process of paying the interest and the agreed amount on the principal.

But as I said, that's getting into more sophisticated borrowing. It is essential, however, if you go into business to have a credit line. I don't think you can have too much credit available to you, if you know how to use it responsibly.

The other thing I want to talk about on the subject of credit is debt. Obviously, debt is what you get when you get credit. As far as I'm concerned, there are two kinds of debt—good debt and bad debt.

Bad debt is buying things above your means, such as expensive cars, clothing, jewelry, and all kinds of stuff that won't bring you any return.

Spending your money "fast and loose" on these kinds of items is a sure way to go speeding to the poor house. While these things may be nice to look at, and even nice to own (when you're able to do so without spending your income on them) remember that buying expensive items such as these is not going to do you any good financially. So be mindful of this fact whenever you find yourself tempted to spend money on such things.

Today, most people (especially those living away from the large, urban northeast cities) prefer private transportation to get around. Even though this is true, it does not mean you have to have a Mercedes, a Hummer H2, a Lexus, or a Cadillac. Now these are all very fine vehicles. Even a Rolls Royce or a Bentley is OK, if and when you're able to purchase them. But until you are able to do this, I recommend comfortable yet reliable basic transportation that will be adequate for getting you from point A to point B. I consider it to be bad debt when you over extend yourself with burdensome car notes trying to make a luxury statement that your income cannot support. That's living beyond your means, and it's abuse of the credit privilege. It is also a good example of a lifestyle being lived for "appearances only," and usually the one living it is only fooling him or her self. Don't let a situation such as this be yours if you really want to become wealthy. Trust me, this is not the road to wealth, it is the path to the poorhouse.

## The Difference Between "Good Debt" and "Bad Debt"

Some people think of all debt as bad. They often speak of wanting to get their homes paid off, and not wanting to take on any more debts. I hear people say all the time, "I want to be debt free."

It's all right to be debt free. Free of car payments, and even house payments for that matter. That's all fine. But even though you might like to live without debt, still you need to understand that not all debt is bad. The reason you need to understand this is because you can't grow financially strong fast enough just from your savings alone. In fact, you are not going to live long enough to save your way to prosperity. You would have to live to be about 200 years old, in order to save enough money to call yourself wealthy at the rate many Americans save. Therefore, the only way you can begin to amass the kind of money you need to become financially independent is through the use of debt!

Now, this opens the door for my discussion about "good debt." Good debt is going into debt for the purpose of investing—whether it is to purchase stocks, bonds, real estate, or any other form of investment that will give you an adequate return. Good debt is actually quite excellent, because it allows you to buy more. It's what is called "leverage." What is leverage?

The first time I heard this word used was with an old professor when I was in college. He said, "Do y'all know what a seesaw is? OK, have you ever seen a little guy on one side of a seesaw, and a big guy on the other side? If they're equal distance from the middle, who is going to pick up whom?"

We answered, "If they both get on each end of that seesaw, then the little one better watch out, because he is going to fly high up in the air."

Then the old professor said, "But suppose this little fellow has a block of cement on his side which is heavier than the big guy on the other end, then he will raise that guy."

The professor was right. The little guy would indeed be able to lift up the big guy with the help of the extra weight. That's the way leverage works in the financial arena. Let's say you have $10,000. If you wanted to leverage the $10,000 to get $100,000, here is how you can do it. You could put the $10,000 into a piece of real estate valued at $100,000, and then borrow $90,000 using the property as collateral. Now you have $100,000 out there working for you.

Why is that important? Well, it's simple. If the return on $100,000 were 10%, that is $10,000 you would earn. If that $10,000 has a return of 10%, you'd earn $1,000. So you multiplied your abilities to earn and control wealth by 10 times.

That's what leverage is. But unless you maintain good credit so that you are able to borrow, you cannot accomplish the leveraging feat. That is really the ultimate result of starting out in life with good credit, then expanding it to be able to acquire additional credit through the use of good debt.

Of course you should save. But remember this: It is that second house as an investment, buying that piece of land, buying that apartment building or shopping strip, buying stocks or bonds, etc., and borrowing the money with which to do it, that's going to make you wealthy. Still, just as you must guard your credit, you must also guard against becoming over leveraged. The reason for this is because in bad economic times, the multiplier effect is reversed.

If you can remember to guard against overextending yourself financially, and to borrow amounts of money that you can easily pay back, controlling both your debts and your assets, your chance of becoming financially independent is much greater. It's simple. It's easy. And I truly believe any disciplined working American can do it.

If you have desire and determination, you can work and save your money. If you are disciplined, you're going to be able to establish good credit, repay your debts, and reach your goal of financial independence. But if you have a goal to go nowhere, you will certainly arrive there on or ahead of time. And if you don't set challenging goals, you'll achieve "nothing" according to plan.

Remember: The biggest barrier to financial independence is that people don't plan enough, and those who do plan often don't <u>follow up</u> on their plans with disciplined commitment.

In closing, I want to reiterate to you how important it is to try to avoid having to take drastic actions—such as bankruptcy, to solve your credit problems. As you begin to develop better credit habits, you'll begin to enjoy the fruits of good credit behavior. To get you started on a plan that will enable you to begin establishing and maintaining good credit, here is a simple formula that can help, if you choose to follow it:

| | |
|---|---|
| 1. Save one-tenth of your income | 10% |
| 2. Give one-tenth to charity | 10% |
| 3. Pay your creditors four-tenths of your income | 40% |
| 3. Live on four-tenths of your income | 40% |
| **Total** | **100%** |

Use this formula whenever you are making a purchase. If the purchase places you outside of this formula, you know that you have gone too far. Make it a habit, beginning today, to buy no more than you can pay for using your current income. No matter what you've done in the past, think of today as a new day. It's your chance to start over. To get it right. Now, please read the chapter on credit again.

## *Summary of Step 5*
## Establish Good Credit

This step is a bridge. It lies between your old habits and your new possibilities. I cannot emphasize to you enough the value of good credit to becoming a millionaire. The good news is that even if your credit has suffered in the past, you can still redeem it. You are not a lost cause. But you must begin today, right now. And you must stay the course. Once you do this, you are creating a bridge from your old lifestyle, to your new lifestyle—the one leading you to the financial independence you want, need, and deserve. In fact, I would like you to get up right now, and go and look in the mirror. I hope the person staring back at you is a new person, with a new and better financial outlook.

*Step 6*

# Just Say "No" to Renting—
# Purchase Your Home

Home ownership is the next vital step you'll need to take on your path to becoming a millionaire.

Now, if you already own your own home, this chapter may seem like I'm preaching to the choir. I say this because if you're already a homeowner, it's clear you already realize it is much better to buy your residence, than to rent it. Still, I want to encourage you to read this chapter, because it will reaffirm for you the wisdom of the decision you made to purchase your home. It might also provide you with a viewpoint you can share with loved ones and friends who are still renting.

For those who have not yet purchased a home, let me tell you now that home ownership is absolutely *essential* to using my method of becoming a millionaire. You need to own the place where you live. Whether you are a single working person or someone with a family, you should purchase real estate for the purpose of providing shelter for yourself and/or for you and your family.

What does owning your own home have to do with helping to increase and secure greater financial freedom on the way to becoming a millionaire?

1. Owning your own home means you can have more control over your immediate environment. When you can control important aspects of your immediate environment, you can free your mind, allowing you to spend quality time thinking and planning for your financial future.

2. When you can manage your financial life so that you can own the place where you live, it is likely you will develop and activate skills allowing you to better manage other aspects of your finances.

3. A home represents a sound investment. Once you build up equity in the home you own, you can use the equity to help you secure funds for investment in other property or for other investments that can help insure your financial freedom on the road to becoming a millionaire. Because you can use your home's equity, ownership is also a sort of "forced" savings plan (but should not replace your regular savings plan).

4. Going through the "process" involved in purchasing a home educates you in financial matters. You can then use your "home-buying education" to seek out and find other wealth-building opportunities. Conquering your fear of financial matters will enable you to become better prepared, intellectually, to seek even greater financial freedom.

5. A home means you can experience peace of mind and joy in a place of refuge that only ownership can offer you. After all, home ownership is the best (and most valued) part of the American dream.

## You Need Control Over Your Immediate Environment

There is no doubt that far too many families are still being reared in rental units. There is also little doubt that many landlords and rental unit managers take apartment-dwelling people for granted, knowing there will always be a steady supply of renters. Because this is the case, a lot of these places are often unfit for human habitation, while others are poorly managed, and most cost too much.

When you're renting, you have no control over what your neighbors do. In most instances, there is only a thin wall—above, below, and all around you—separating you and your closest neighbors. That means you can hear, often with great clarity, their music, their loud conversations, their arguments, and in the worst situations, their bathroom usage. Owning a home, therefore, can provide a sanctuary where you have more control over what you have to listen to in your intimate surroundings. Home ownership also includes single-family condominiums and townhomes.

I believe home ownership is essential, especially for families. I believe all children should have a decent and safe place in which to learn, grow, and play, and that parents should do all they can to provide such a dwelling place for their children. Furthermore, I am confident it is entirely possible for any individual or family now living in an apartment to own a home.

After all, if you're renting, somehow you are managing to pay the rent each month. It doesn't matter if you're managing your finances using only your own income, or if you're supplementing it with some kind of government subsidy. Still, you are meeting your monthly rental obligation. Since you are able to do this, it is possible that you may be able to purchase a home. Remember, there is no reason for a "permanent underclass" to exist in America. There is also no reason you should be a part of one if it does exist. You can "move up" in America. If you have an income stream, you are probably able to purchase a home. Now, you're going to have to budget wisely in order to save up money for a down payment, but the "payoff," your own home, should be more than enough enticement for you to start a savings program. (Let me encourage you to go back and re-read Chapter 2, the chapter on developing a savings habit, to begin getting yourself into the mindset needed for setting aside your down payment for your new home.)

## Equity For You, Or For Your Landlord?

Simply stated, it pays to learn to manage your finances. Being a homeowner means you have learned what it takes to meet the obligations of ownership.

Remember, it doesn't matter how long you pay rent, your rent payments will continue until death. Now, contrast the rent-paying process with that of buying a home. One thing is certain, when you are a homeowner, if you keep making those mortgage payments month after month and year after year, one day it will be paid for in full.

The only certainty about renting is that your monthly rental payments *will increase,* while at some point in your life the income to support that payment will decline—and, in some cases, it will stop completely. It is also a rental certainty that a landlord (or property manager) will decide when you must pay higher rent or move, and that your landlord or property owner will surely grow wealthy from the income and equity he builds up in the property you're paying to live in.

With this in mind, I believe the choice is clear. You can continue to help your landlord grow richer and richer by keeping his income stream increasing steadily from year to year, or you can look into home ownership. I hope you'll make the wise choice.

## A Home Represents a Sound Investment

A home affords numerous benefits to its owner, other than simply providing shelter. First of all, a home represents a good, sound financial investment. Next, it belongs to you, and it is yours to decorate and make as comfortable or as elegant as you like. You don't have to ask anyone's permission to paint the walls or put up wallpaper, because it is yours, and you can fix it up based on your own tastes and preferences.

A home can also offer a safe place in which to rear a family by providing children a better environment in which to grow. Although crime can occur anywhere, in a good neighborhood, you're less likely to be subjected to a living environment you have no control over, as is often the case in apartment living. A home is also a financial safety net, of sorts. This is true because as you pay your mortgage, and as your home increases in value, you are building "equity" in your investment.

The equity in your home increases your net worth and may be used by you for any legal purpose you may choose. This includes using your home as security for a loan.

According to Fannie Mae's 2003 National Housing Survey (Fannie Mae is a government-sponsored housing finance company), most (87 percent) homeowners believe their homes value has increased since they first purchased, and 76 percent believe their home is now worth more than they expected.

In fact, historically, home ownership has proven to be a sound and sensible investment. I am convinced this will be true for many years to come, and probably forever, simply because the population of the U.S. and the world will continue to grow, creating increased demand on our fixed supply of land and affordable, adequate housing.

For this reason, real estate will always be a good investment. Elementary economics teaches that if there is a fixed supply of anything and the demand for it increases, the price will rise. Therefore, not only is a home a good and safe place to raise a family, it is also an excellent investment that will become more valuable over the years.

Buying a home is not a back burner proposition. It is something that should be accomplished as soon as you are financially able.

## Purchasing a Home Helps to "Educate" You About Finance

Going through the *process* of buying a home can only serve to make you smarter, whether you end up with a home or not. At the end of this chapter, I've made a list of steps involved in the process of purchasing a home, from filling out the application, to what you'll need to bring with you when you visit a realtor or mortgage financier. When you look at this list, you will see that you'll have to be ready to divulge a lot of financial information during the home-buying process. In order for this divulgence to be in your favor, you're going to need to account for and/or respond to any perceived weaknesses in the areas covered in these steps.

If you'd like, prior to actually going through the process, you could use the steps I've outlined as a way to experience a "trial run" on your own, to see how your financial picture will develop when you're ready to purchase your first home (or your next home). The process is fairly standard. Therefore, you can use your "education" about what it takes to get financed for a home, to seek out and find other wealth-building opportunities. As I stated earlier, once you conquer your fear of financial matters, you will be better prepared, intellectually, to reach for greater financial freedom.

## Prepare to Experience the Joy of Home Ownership

Nothing feels better than owning your own. It doesn't matter if you're talking about your own car, your own CD player, your own computer, or your own home. It just feels better having something to call your own. As the old Porgy and Bess song attests, "Mama may have, and papa may have, but God bless the child that's got his own." The idea of ownership didn't make it into the song just because it makes for catchy lyrics. It's there because of the truth behind the words. And you cannot know the depth of this truth until you own.

Remember, as a first-time homebuyer, you should not insist on purchasing "the home of your dreams." Why? Because your dream home may be selling at a price you can only afford in your dreams. Instead, I am encouraging you to select the best property you can afford. It may be a home you are not head-over-heels in love with, or one you would not buy if your circumstances were different. But none of this matters at this time. By purchasing a home you can easily afford to pay for, you will be setting a strong foundation for building the kind of wealth you'll need to purchase your dream home later. Staying within a price-range that's easy for you to afford will enable you to make your mortgage payments with no pain every month. Buying out of your range of affordability will undoubtedly leave you strapped for cash every month, and you will be too worried and stressed out about money matters to cultivate other opportunities for building wealth in your life. So, for now—for your first home—you should purchase the best you can afford with the dollars you have. And believe me, the home of your dreams is certainly just around the corner, if you play your cards right.

A home is a wonderful investment that can put you firmly on the path to financial freedom. Following are five important factors of financial freedom that home ownership makes possible:

1. Historically, the increase in value of homes has outperformed the economy and most other stable investments. For this reason, you can most likely expect your home to appreciate in value, allowing you to sell it for more than it cost you.

2. Additionally, a home will afford great emotional gratification, like the healthy pride that comes from owning something of great value. Renting could never offer you this kind of personal fulfillment, because as long as you're renting, you're helping some other person experience this satisfaction.

3. Ultimately, owning a home can help foster an attitude of greater self esteem, more so than any other single item an individual can buy. In fact, I believe nothing can bring more joy and happiness to a working person than to return, after a hard day on the job, to a

home he or she owns. And, since self-esteem is a key ingredient for success and productivity, a person who owns a home is likely to be more self-confident and better prepared to seek different ways of attaining increased financial freedom that are crucial to becoming a millionaire.

4. A homeowner will have a higher standing in the community in which he or she lives. The lending institutions (banks, savings and loan companies, etc.) always look more favorably upon a homeowner's request to borrow money for other worthwhile purposes. And, it just plain *feels good* to own property and to know that owning it boosts your financial standing in the community.

5. In most instances, a home will appreciate and have good or great resale value. If you own a home that does not meet your needs, you don't have to hesitate to sell it and buy another one, once you can afford to do so. Whether you're seeking a bigger home in a better neighborhood, or you're going after the home of your dreams, you can sell or lease your present home in order to buy another one.

## Home Buying 101

Since home ownership is a vital step on the path to becoming a millionaire, it is very important to address in this book the process of buying a home for the first time. People who have never purchased a home, I believe, need to be walked carefully and caringly through the process in order to gain greater understanding of what it actually entails. Becoming educated about the home-buying process makes it easier for renters to imagine home ownership. And, after all, being able to *imagine* home ownership is truly the first step in the home-buying process.

Ultimately, it is my goal to put at ease readers who have not yet purchased a home, who now realize the importance of this step on the way to becoming a millionaire.

Later in this chapter, my emphasis will shift to investing in single-family homes as a way to gain greater financial freedom. But the point I'm making now is that the purchase of a home as something that will provide shelter for you and your family is one of the most vital steps on the path to financial freedom. After all, every plan has to begin somewhere, and a home of your own is a most logical place to start investing in your future.

How do you get that first home? In previous chapters, we have discussed the importance of education and training, job stability, credit, and the kinds of things you should do to prepare yourself to get to this point. Once you have prepared yourself in these other ways, and you arrive at the point where you are ready to buy a first home, then you're ready for the advice this chapter contains.

When it comes to purchasing your first home, you can choose to do it yourself, or you can seek the help and advice of a real estate professional. There's no doubt in my mind there are many people who can go out alone and do all the work associated with purchasing a home. But it is my recommendation that you work with a real estate agent.

With this in mind, you'll need to decide which real estate company you will use. To select your real estate company and agent, you will need to narrow down the number of neighborhoods you're willing to consider living in. I'm sure you will make your neighborhood selections based on such criteria as whether there are good schools (if you have children), a low incidence of crime, shopping considerations, or other considerations and/or amenities important to you in selecting the area where you'll live.

Next, you're ready to interview a real estate agent. In this interview, you will tell the agent the type of home you would like to own, and the kind of neighborhood you want to live in. You're also going to have to answer all the financial questions relative to your income, credit, etc.

In this session, the agent is going to interview you, and you're going to interview the agent. The interview will provide a brief glimpse into the agent's business style and personal character, helping you decide whether or not you'd like to work with him or her. If for some reason you feel you are not compatible with the agent you've interviewed, you can elect to switch agents in that same firm, or you can choose to go to another firm. Remember, you are looking for someone in whom you can have confidence; someone who is going to look for the best home-buying opportunity for you.

When you set out to find the best real estate agent for you, keep in mind you'll need one that will always consider your best interest. For that reason, it might be helpful to begin your agent search by asking friends, relatives, and coworkers for referrals. There may be many companies and agencies to choose from in the area where you would like to purchase your home, and you'll need all the help you can get to narrow the field. You might also consider going to the Internet. Most real estate companies and agents will have a Web site where you will be able to find a lot of the information you'll need when buying a home, as well as information to help you select a real estate agent or company.

After narrowing the field, you should interview two or three agents, face-to-face. Make sure you let the agent know your level of experience with home buying. It will be helpful for them to know if this is your first time buying, or that you have bought a home before. Your choice of agent should be based on your perceived level of comfort with and trust in the people you interview. If you're not comfortable talking to the person, asking questions, and getting the answers you need, then you may need to continue your search for the right agent. Remember, the real estate agent is going to be the most important member of your home-buying team. The agent you choose should be able to help you:

1. Determine exactly what you want in a home.
2. Ascertain your price range.
3. Learn more about your community of choice, providing information on things such as the average price of homes, quality of schools, property taxes, community services, and other characteristics of neighborhoods and homes in the area you want to live in.
4. Offer advice regarding mortgage lending, the appraisal and inspection processes, a list of title companies and insurance companies.
5. Draw up your contract to purchase and present your offer to the seller.

Your agent should have access to the Multiple Listing Service (MLS). This is a service that provides realtors with access to just about all homes for sale in any area you choose to live.

Most of the time, the seller pays the real estate agent. When a home is put on the market, the agent acquiring that property for selling is referred to as the "listing agent." The seller agrees to pay the listing agent a percentage of the sale price. The listing agent agrees to pay the agent for the buyer, usually half of the commission that is generated from the sale of the home.

How will you know when you have selected the right agent? What are some of the key indications that this is the agent who will work best with you and for you? Here are some of the primary characteristics of an agent concerned about your best interest:

- The right agent will be friendly, making you feel "at ease" in their presence, and will promptly address any and all of your real estate related problems and concerns.
- He or she will share insights with you with regard to the housing market, and to the neighborhoods you're interested in, making you feel your best interest is being looked out for as you attempt to achieve your ultimate goal of buying real estate.
- The best agent for you will ask you the right questions in an effort to address your concerns and solve any problems related to the particular property you want to purchase, the neighborhood you're interested in, and the amenities you want in your home and in your neighborhood.
- You should feel that the agent is more interested in helping you select the best home for you, than he or she is in getting you into a contract solely for the purpose of receiving a commission. While it is true that the agent has to be concerned about making a commission since his or her "bread and butter" is paid for through the sale of real estate, still, if commissions appear to be the only thing that interests the agent, then you need another agent more concerned about serving customers.

A good real estate agent will probably show you three homes—maybe a few more, or a few less. If you are honest with the agent about what it is you want, and about your true capacity to buy, the agent should not have to show you hundreds of homes in order to find the home you want. If the initial interview is conducted properly, and you give the agent all the correct information, chances are, within a very few days (and sometimes even on the first day), the agent can help you locate your new home. And when the agent you select finds the property that best fits your needs and your budget, you should not hesitate to make your purchasing decision.

I say this, because it seems sometimes people labor under the false impression that "We found this too soon." Or that "There must be something better out there."

Now it will always be quite possible that there's something better out there, no matter what home you choose. But if you are truly working with the right agent for your needs, the reason you will be able to find a property fairly quickly is that the agent has taken time to get to know you and your needs, and he or she is simply using expert knowledge to find your new home. The right agent for you knows what he or she is doing. In fact, when you're ready to purchase, and you're working with the right agent, it shouldn't take a long time to find the property you want.

After the property is found, you will be asked to make a commitment by signing a contract making an initial offer. I know that's a hard decision sometimes because when you are signing your name, you are creating a legal, binding document. But if you are sincere about purchasing a home, you should know there are legalities involved in the home-buying process.

If you have located a property and are ready to make an offer on it, your next question should be "How much should I pay for that property?"

While you should not depend solely on having your agent tell you what to pay for a property, the agent will help you in your decision-making about how much to pay. How? By providing you with a market analysis giving an estimate of the true value of the property.

If the property is on the market at a fair market price, then you might consider making an offer of five percent below what the property is worth. Of course, if the seller counters with another price, and you are convinced that the house is a good buy, then you should probably pay the price. Too many people have lost good properties in good neighborhoods because they couldn't get the people to come down on the price.

The fact is, sometimes there will be excellent properties on the market for the right price, and no good reason for the seller to reduce the price in order to sell the property. As a potential buyer, you could possibly miss out on a good buy if you haggle too much over a price that truly is reasonable.

Of course, I would advise anyone to try to reduce the price of a property just to save some money. And the odds are great that almost every property on the market is probably listed for a little more than the owner will actually take for the property. So I'm not saying you should just pay the list price for the property you want. I am saying, however, that you should have a good idea about the prices and market values of homes in your range of affordability. When you know this, it will become much easier for you to make a good decision quickly about what your purchase price should be. Helping buyers determine the value of the homes they are purchasing is one of the real estate agent's most important jobs.

Chances are, before you make an offer on the house and have it accepted; you will go over the financing you will use to get the property, because that will determine the type of contract you will write.

A first-time homebuyer will probably not have sufficient funds to assume a mortgage. More often than not, he or she is looking to put a minimum amount down on a home and borrow the rest from an institutional lender. In this instance, the buyer has three alternatives: VA, FHA, and Conventional financing.

## A Close Look at Financing Alternatives

In the past, people looking to purchase a home found the home first, then the financing. Today, people get approved for financing before looking for a home. For now, let's look at three major financing options: VA, FHA, and Conventional loans. Later in this chapter, I will delve more deeply into other financing considerations.

Let's begin this discussion with VA financing. Most of you reading this book will not fall into the eligible category for VA financing. VA loans or Veteran Administration backed loans are designed to accommodate those who have served in the Armed Services, and have been honorably discharged or are presently in the military serving their country. Those who have served our country as service men and women, however, should definitely pay close attention to this information (and they should seek further information on this topic). As time goes by, the maximum loan amount for VA guaranteed loans increases, because the price of properties becomes more expensive.

At this time (year 2006), the VA guarantees a maximum of 25% of a home loan amount up to $60,000 (valoans.com). The maximum VA home loan amount is $359,650, with no down payment required from the buyer. This includes a funding fee that is rolled into the loan. Veterans qualify based on use of a residual income method, which refers to the veteran's net or extra income remaining after all housing and living expenses have been paid.

Federal Housing Administration (FHA) loans also utilize the residual income approach. This is done in an effort to qualify buyers who are unable to qualify based on its lenient income to debt ratios. FHA downpayments are normally lower than those for conventional loans, with some as low as three percent.

Conventional financing requires a minimum of five percent down and the other costs to close are generally higher than those for FHA and VA financing. These loans use the income to debt ratio approach and their qualifying criteria are usually more stringent than FHA requirements. Conventional loans usually include "due on sale clauses" which prohibit the owner from selling the home on an assumption. The balance must be paid before a sale, unless the purchaser gets the approval of the mortgage company. The conventional loan is one that is not backed by the government. This type of loan usually requires a 5% (or higher) down payment. However, of late, we are experiencing a relatively new twist to this type of financing—that is, the granting of this loan with no money down. Yes, zero—nothing—no money out of the purchaser's pocket. For the most part, to qualify for a loan like this you must have very good credit. We closed a loan like this recently for one of our customers, and the purchaser, after having put no money into the transaction, walked away from the closing table with over $300.00 to put in his pocket.

## Home Inspection Time

Another professional important to your home purchase process is the residential inspector, or inspection firm, conducting the inspection of the property you want to buy. The purpose of the inspection is not just to point out what is wrong with a piece of property because almost every property is going to have some type of problem. You need the home inspection for the purpose of:

1. Understanding the condition of the home you're buying, so you'll know exactly what it is that you're getting for your money.
2. Making sure there are no major problems hidden from even the seller or agent.
3. Making sure there are no problems that may not be easily identified as problems.

The professional inspector may be able to find the kind of problem that is better to have been discovered before you buy the property. Even after finding a major problem, you might decide it is still in your best interest to buy, but at least you won't be surprised six months after purchase with the need to spend money for a new roof, or to level the foundation. Home inspectors are among the list of professionals you need to help you purchase your first home. In some states, such as Texas, home inspectors are required to be licensed through the state.

After the inspection, you may renegotiate with the owner to take care of some repairs. They may choose to provide money for a "repair allowance," or reduce the price of the home so that you can take care of the repairs. In some cases, it may be that the inspection will uncover defects causing you not to purchase a particular home.

## "Walk-Through" the Steps of the Home-Buying Process

Finally, let us take a "virtual" walk-through of the nine basic steps involved in purchasing a home. It is important that you consider each step carefully, so that you will be well prepared when you're ready to purchase your home. While each step seems basic and simple, there is more to each than meets the eye. It may appear to be easy, for example, to "select a realtor." But if you remember the cautions I mentioned earlier in this chapter, you know this selection process should address your general and particular needs and desires.

1. **Locate a real estate agent.** An agent can help you determine what you really want and can afford.
2. **Make a loan application with a mortgage company.** Select your own mortgage company or ask your real estate agent to help you select one.

3. **Find your new home.** Shop for the home that meets your needs, or for your dream home if you can afford it. Your agent can show you homes that fit your lifestyle and your budget.

4. **Write a contract to purchase the property.** Your agent will help you write the contract.

5. **Negotiate the contract.** You and the seller must agree on the terms of the contract to finalize the offer. When you and the seller agree on terms, you have a legal binding contract that you can now use to purchase the property.

6. **Wait for your loan to be finalized with the mortgage company.** This process usually takes from 30 minutes to 10 days. If you have good credit, a stable job, and cash for a down payment, you could be approved in as little time as 30 minutes. On the other hand, if you have "challenged" credit and/or other financial problems, the approval process could take weeks. An underwriter will review your credit, job stability, income, debt, and savings to determine if you qualify for a mortgage. Additionally, the mortgage company will order an appraisal to establish market value of the home you are purchasing.

7. **Once your loan has been approved, you will need to order a termite and residential home inspection**. If the inspection reveals that repairs are needed, or if you and the seller agree on repairs to be made, the repairs must be made prior to closing. Closing is when you will sign all of the documents, pay your money, and take title to your new home.

8. **Closing**. Once inspections and repairs have been made, you will make an appointment to close with the title company.

9. **End of process.** After funding and closing, you are finally ready to move into your new home. All parties involved in the purchase have been paid.

## Locating Financing for Real Property

In this section, we're going to look more intently at different kinds of financing options available to people purchasing homes. This information will help you get a firm grip on understanding financial considerations if you are purchasing your first home to live in, or if you've arrived at a point where you can purchase homes or other kinds of real estate as investment property. Since it is highly likely that any purchase of real estate will get you farther down the path toward becoming a millionaire, it is vital that you understand financing as well as possible.

Millions of Americans have been scared out of the housing market by the complicated financing techniques available today in the marketplace. Many professionals operating in the field—and even the news media—have commented about the mind-boggling concoction of alphabet soup characterizing financing programs. Even though it is a topic terrifying to many, I will work hard in this section of this book to make it clear that there is no need to be frightened by complicated financing techniques. To make my point, I will set down a few rules you can follow that will help guide you through a financing transaction. It can be complicated, of course, but all kinds of homebuyers have navigated these waters time and again and have successfully financed their homes. And if they can do it, so can you. With this in mind, I'm presenting the advice in this section for first or second time homebuyers, and to the beginning investor in real estate.

There are numerous types of financing programs in the marketplace, and I don't think it would be wise or ultimately beneficial for me to describe and explain all the methods or techniques available today. Instead, I will focus on four of the most frequently used financing instruments. They are:

1. Government insured and guaranteed loans. These include FHA (Federal Housing Administration) and VA (Veterans Administration)
2. Conventional loans
3. Wraparound financing
4. Contract for Deed, Installment Sale, or Land Contract

## FHA Insured Mortgage

The FHA loan is another option for purchasing residential property meeting certain criteria. The Federal Housing Administration (FHA) was created in 1934 by an Act of Congress to encourage the construction and ownership of homes, especially those in the lower price range. Under this Act, borrowers may obtain loans up to 97% of the value of the home that may be either new construction or an existing home. The home, of course, must meet the requirements of the FHA. These loans on residential properties may be made on terms up to 30 years. The Act has been amended and changed a number of times since its inception, but the FHA loan still remains. It is one of the most popular forms of financing for most people who are buying homes in the medium and the low price range.

In terms of loans requiring 5% or less as a down payment, FHA-insured loans are the easiest type to qualify for. This is true because the guidelines for loan qualification are more flexible than any other type of mortgage loans with similar down payment requirements. The Web site fha.com (in 2005) listed some of the basic guidelines for qualifying for an FHA-insured loan. These include:

- Steady employment. (At least two years, preferably with same employer.)
- Steady income. (The last two years of your income should be the same or showing an increase in earnings.)
- Steady bill payment history. (Your credit report should show that you've been paying your bills on time, with fewer than two incidences of 30-day late payments in the last two years.)
- No recent bankruptcy. (If you have a bankruptcy, it must be at least two years since you filed, and your credit must be good since you filed.)
- No recent foreclosure. (If you have a foreclosure in your credit report, it has to be at least three years old, and your record must show good credit since the foreclosure.)
- Must meet mortgage payment-to-income ratio requirements. (Your mortgage payment will have to be, approximately, within 30% of your gross income.)

The thing that is so important about the FHA loan is that it allows the purchaser of a home to acquire the home with a low down payment, especially when you use what is called the acquisition cost method.

The acquisition cost is the lesser of the sale price or value of the property plus closing costs paid by the purchaser, excluding prepaid items. For owner occupied properties, the loan amount is based on 97% of the first $25,000 and 95% of the amount over $25,000. For investors buying these properties the maximum mortgage is 85% of the acquisition cost.

The Federal Housing Administration 203(b) mortgage plan is now the most commonly used HUD program for insuring the purchase of single-family homes. Section 203(b) may be used to purchase a new or existing one to four-family home, and it is available all over the nation, in rural and urban areas. A home must meet HUD's Minimum Property Standards, and the mortgage may be repaid in monthly installments over a period of 10, 15, 20, 25, or 30 years.

Under the 203(b) program, there are special terms available to qualified veterans desiring to purchase a single-family home. It provides financing for up to 100% of the first $25,000 and 95% financing of the amount over $25,000. If the property is less than one year old, and was built without FHA/VA inspections and cannot be covered by HOW warranty, the loan will be limited to 90% of acquisition cost. Of course, the veteran must have served at least 90 consecutive days active duty or have a certificate issued by the Secretary of Defense establishing extra hazardous duty for service less than 90 days. He must have been discharged under conditions other than dishonorable. This loan does not require the use of credit scoring, and there is no limit on the number of times eligibility can be used in FHA programs (after he or she presents a Certificate of Veterans Status from the Department of Veterans Affairs).

Another popular FHA loan has a minimum down payment requirement of 3%, and allows the borrower to receive as a gift (from a relative, nonprofit organization or government agency) all of the money needed at closing.

## *Spotlight: The FHA "Reverse" Mortgage*

There have always been a lot of good financial reasons to purchase a home. One more safety net was added, however, when the FHA adopted the Reverse Mortgage Loan. A truly unique product, it actually sounds too good to be true.

First of all, there are no financial qualifications for this mortgage. The

FHA does not look at credit scores, debt ratios or income. The only qualification is that the borrower must be at least 62 years old, and the property must be their primary residence. Secondly, any homeowner meeting this requirement can borrow against the home's value, and not have to pay the money back within his or her lifetime. How can this be? It is possible because the heirs of the borrower are responsible for repayment of the debt. And lastly, but certainly not least, once a homeowner obtains a reverse mortgage, s/he never has to make monthly payments on it—ever. The usual monthly interest and principal are deferred for the life of the homeowner. That means the mortgage only becomes due and payable when one of three things happens:

1. The homeowner sells the property.
2. The homeowner moves away from the property for more than two months.
3. The homeowner dies.

If there is more than one borrower and one of them precedes the other in death, nothing happens. The mortgage continues and no payment is due. When the surviving owner dies, title to the property is then transferred to the heirs of the estate who then have up to 12 months (one year) to decide what to do with the house. During the 12 months, heirs are not required to make payments.

Homeowners receiving loan proceeds from the reverse mortgage can choose to either have the funds paid in a lump sum following closing, receive equal monthly payments for life, or establish a line of credit from which to draw funds as long as they are needed. (The line of credit option is not available in Texas.) These loans are highly regulated and are, therefore, basically the same everywhere.

The Reverse Mortgage is truly one of the best benefits to home ownership. I like to call programs such as this one **Money From Home**.

## VA Loans

Those who have served our country through the military may choose to apply for the VA loan. The proper name for the Veterans Administration loan is GI Guaranteed Mortgage, but it is better known as the VA loan.

Under the Serviceman's Readjustment Act of 1940 (which has been amended a number of times), eligible veterans and unmarried widows of veterans who died in the service (or of service connected causes) can obtain a guaranteed loan for the purchase or construction of their home. Although the Veterans Administration verifies eligibility it does not actually lend money. Rather, it guarantees loans made to qualified applicants by lending institutions.

The guarantee entitlement for veterans started on April 20, 1950, and the amount of the guarantee was $4,000. It has been raised many times since then. In year 2001, full entitlement was $60,000. What that really amounts to is that the Veterans Administration guarantees to the lender $60,000 of a veteran's loan, even if the he or she defaults on the mortgage. This guarantee enables the veteran to get the loan without paying any type of down payment. In 2005, the maximum amount of the loan was raised to $359,650. Any loan above this amount requires that down payment arrangements be made with the lender on the amount in excess of $359,650.

To determine eligibility for a VA loan guarantee, applicants must submit certain documents and follow certain application procedures. Just as with other kinds of loans, the veteran must have the necessary income and credit worthiness to get a loan. Like any borrower, he or she must show the same ability to pay back the loan as the primary condition for granting the loan.

## Conventional Loan

The conventional loan is a loan for the purchase of a home that is not backed by a government guarantee or that is not government insured. These loans are generally called "80% loans," meaning the purchaser must come up with a 20% down payment. Generally this gives the buyer the interest rates available in the market place. There are always some exceptions that you can find throughout the country, but generally, if you pay 20% down you can get the best interest rate. For the most part, down payments of more than 20%, such as 30% or 40% still may not increase your chances of getting a better interest rate.

Then there is the 90% loan, which requires a 10% down payment.

Usually with this loan you will have to get private mortgage insurance. The private mortgage insurance companies provide guarantees similar to FHA and VA. With this loan, private insurance companies are guaranteeing the loan. They will guarantee a certain percentage of that loan up to 20%.

Last, there is the crème de la crème of financing options—the 95% to 100% loan. Almost all lenders, including savings and loans institutions, require private mortgage insurance on these loans. This kind of financing is much more difficult to come by because the borrower must have a very good credit record and the house must appraise at the selling price or above, without any problems. Also of great importance are the borrower's debt ratios, which must be well within the range of what is considered standard for a "good" loan. But the 95% or 100% loan is still available in the marketplace for those who can qualify for it.

There's not a whole lot more to say about conventional loans, other than the fact that they give you a variety of options. You are pretty much limited to the imagination of the lender and the borrower as to how these loans can be arranged and set up. Almost any lending institution may make this type of loan. Historically, the savings and loans institutions have led in making conventional mortgage loans. In recent years we've seen an increase in the number of banks and other institutions making conventional loans. Today some of the new "interest only" and other loan products allow lower monthly payments than is necessary to fully amortize (pay off) the loan. These products often keep the loan balance the same or the outstanding balance may increase. While these types of loans have gained in popularity, my advice is that you stay away from them.

## Wraparound Mortgages

A man came to my office one day, and before his bottom could hit the seat I gave him, he said to me, "I've got a BIG problem." I smiled at him and said something like "You know, this is a beautiful day the Lord has made for golf." He looked at me as if I had turned into the forked-tail devil. Then there was only silence in the room as we both looked out of the window for one minute that seemed much longer. Finally, the man couldn't stand the silence, so he asked if I had heard what he said. I looked at him. Then he revamped with even more urgency his original statement, "I got ONE HELL of a problem." I looked at him calmly and said, "I can tell you have a serious problem, but let me tell you there is no problem in the world so big that it can't be handled with the help of the Lord." I looked toward the window again, and so did he. We stared at the sun shining everywhere on what was a very beautiful day. In an instant, the man began to calm down. After the transformation of his mood I said to him, "Now, tell me about the problem you have."

The lesson of this incident is that sometimes any of us can get so caught up in our problems that it seems even the wonder and beauty of God's creations cannot get through to us to remind us about all He has given us on earth beyond any material things. But I managed to stop at least one man in his tracks that day, to remind him that even though things in his life might have seemed dark, that he still needed to be looking towards the light.

His problem was that his mortgage company had foreclosed on his house, and he wanted to know why this had happened. We talked about it, and I discovered he had bought his home three and a half years earlier by taking over someone else's loan. But this man had made every payment to the mortgage company, and he had made them on time. I realized then that what we were dealing with was most likely what is called a "wraparound" mortgage.

A wrap around note is one where the original loan remains on the property and the seller finances the property for the buyer by making the buyer a loan that is larger than the original loan, and usually at a higher interest rate. That means the new "wraparound" payments will be larger than the original loan payments. The seller receives the payments from the buyer and makes payments to the mortgage company, keeping the rest of the money.

In this man's case, the sellers had stopped paying the mortgage company and did not let the buyer know, and the mortgage company had never been informed that the home had been sold. I know this sounds as though it should be illegal, but it is not. Using the proper safeguards and a good lawyer, you could safely purchase a home using this method. Still, I would never recommend buying a home using the wraparound mortgage.

The wraparound mortgage has been around for a long time, but until recently, it had been used primarily in commercial transactions. For a few years in the early 80s, interest rates went so high that borrowers could not afford to go to a savings and loan or bank to borrow money for a home. During that time people had to be creative in figuring out a way to get loans and to purchase homes.

Using the wraparound method of financing, the purchaser can buy property, paying the down payment. The seller can then carry a loan that is wrapped around the existing loan. Ideally, the seller makes payments on the existing loan after receiving payments from the buyer on the loan the buyer has made. In effect, the buyer's new loan is "wrapped around" the seller's old loan.

For example, let's say you purchased a home for $150,000 and the outstanding loan on the property was $100,000. To use the wraparound method, an individual would pay to the seller 10% down or $15,000. The seller would give him back a note of $135,000 and each month the purchaser would pay the seller on this $135,000 loan. The seller in turn would pay to the mortgage lender holding the initial loan the amount that is due until the note is satisfied.

In years past the FHA/VA loan could be assumed without any qualifications, and many conventional loans could, until the last few years, be assumed without a "due on sale" clause. A due on sale clause is a section put into the deed of trust requiring the note to be paid off in full if the property is sold. Therefore, when there is such a clause in a particular deed of trust, and the buyer assumes or "wraps" that loan, the buyer is subject to the lender calling that note. There is one thing you must be careful about when taking on a wraparound loan. You must be absolutely sure there is not a "due on sale" clause in the underlying note.

## Contract for Deed, or Land Contract

The last type of loan is referred to as a contract for deed, or a land contract. This kind of loan may be described as one where the deed is not transferred to the buyer until some agreed upon time in the future. Upon the sale of property, a seller may or may not collect a down payment from a purchaser. The decision about whether and when to do this is up to the seller. The seller then agrees to lend or carry back the note on the property, but the deed will not be transferred at the closing. Instead, the seller makes a deed transfer at some time in the future.

Let's take a closer look at how this type of financing works. Let's use, for example, a situation where it is stated that title will be transferred to the purchaser when the purchaser makes a down payment, or has made enough payments to equal 10%, 20%, or 30% of the property's selling price. Or it could be stated that the deed would be transferred when the property has been paid for in full.

The key element of this kind of transaction is that the title of the property remains in the name of the seller for some specified period of time or any combination of time until the property is paid for in full. There is a danger in this kind of purchase because the property is in the name of the seller. If the seller has legal problems or bankruptcy or any other problems, this could affect the transfer of title to the purchaser. In fact there could be things that could occur that would cause the seller to have extreme difficulty transferring title, or that could preclude him from ever being able to do it during the predetermined time in the contract. One danger I have seen occur in this kind of situation is when the seller sells the property to another party, then goes out and borrows money against the property, creating a lien on it. When the time comes to grant the title to the purchaser, he has to satisfy a debt he has created or he cannot transfer title.

So don't forget, buying property and allowing the title to remain in the seller's name can be dangerous. You should only use this purchase arrangement with the help of a lawyer. My recommendation is that you should not use this type of financing when purchasing your home.

## The Mortgage Application

The mortgage application process may be the most important part of the home-buying process because the way the information is presented will determine whether or not your loan is approved.

When a prospective purchaser makes a loan application, he or she should be prepared to provide the mortgage loan officer with precise information regarding personal employment, assets, and credit history. Incomplete information could cause delay in processing the loan application or even cause the applicant to be denied credit.

The following is an outline of the information necessary to make a complete application. The order in which is it presented has no correlation with the degree of importance. It is very important that all applicable information is taken with you when you go to make an application for a mortgage:

1. A current or previous residence address and zip code for the past 24 months including home phone number.
2. Social security numbers of both applicants.
3. A copy of the fully-executed contract of sale for this transaction signed by all parties, if you have signed a contract.
4. Current and previous employment including addresses and zip codes for the past 24 months, and your business phone number.
5. Information about any stocks or bonds you own.
6. Bank balances and account numbers of each checking, savings, credit union, certificates of deposit, including name, address and zip code.
7. Credit references.
8. All current monthly obligations including the balances, monthly payments, account numbers, name and address of lenders and including a list of all credit cards.
9. Commission applicants: real estate agent, insurance salesman, or other commission sales people must bring two years tax return with all schedules attached and signed, including of course, any W-2s or 1099s, and most recent pay stub showing year to date earnings.
10. For the self-employed: previous and current profit and loss statement, balance sheet on business signed by the purchaser and his accountant or CPA or bookkeeper. Tax return for the previous 24 months signed by purchaser and person who prepared the return.
11. If there are any alimony or child support payments or any payments that you are required to pay under the law and any additional

income, be prepared to verify it. Just to say that you have disability checks or some kind of annuity is not enough. You must prove that you do.

12. Of course if it is a VA or FHA/VA loan, a copy of the DD214 or the certificate of eligibility.

13. Provide the face value for life insurance and cash value.

I cannot stress how important it is to provide this information in a timely manner. This can be the difference between approval and rejection, buying or continuing to rent.

## *Summary of Step 6*
## Become a Homeowner

Owning your own home is a vital part of the "millionaire mindset." If you have a job—a steady income stream, there is no good reason why you should not own your own home. Begin making movement toward ownership. Make an action plan, complete with steps and dates, so that your plan is not just a dream. Adding steps and dates will help make your plan real. Home ownership is going to give you needed control over your finances (because with the right financing plan, your mortgage will not increase over the years, as rent will) and you will have more control over your inner sanctum. Controlling your inner sanctum means the possibility of more contentment and peace in your immediate environment, enabling you to spend more quality time contemplating and considering wealth-building opportunities such as those you'll learn about in this book. Finally, going through the "process" involved in purchasing a home will educate you in financial matters, and your new-found learning will render you better prepared, intellectually, to seek the kind of financial freedom you'll need on the way to becoming a millionaire.

*Step 7*

# Insure Yourself and Protect Your Future

7

What good is a plan for living if something happens that takes you out of this world? What would happen to your family, to your dreams, if you go home too early?

Part of what you are doing today to secure your future, financially, has to involve purchasing insurance. But because it can be related to the idea of being ill or dying, insurance is a topic we don't like to think about, let alone discussing and buying it. However, think about it and discuss it we must.

It can be helpful to think of death as part of the great "Circle of Life." Living, after all, is a process. And once we get the hang of what the process involves, it can become less frightening to think of death, because we can view it as the end of the physical aspects of the living process. If you believe in God, you already believe that the end of physical life is not really the end of life, because God promises believers everlasting life. The Bible, in John 3:16, says: "For God so loved the world that he gave his only begotten Son, that whosoever believeth in him should not perish, but have everlasting life." It can be helpful while we're alive on earth to believe this, because it might actually make it easier for us to take care of our earthly duties, responsibilities, and obligations to our loved ones, when we accept the fact that we're all just here temporarily.

When we truly believe in God's promise, we're not living in denial, hoping that something is going to keep us here forever. And we can accept that we must use the brain God gave us to take care of our families while we're alive, and that includes making provisions for their care after we're surely and dearly departed.

## "A good man leaveth an inheritance to his children's children"

As a God-fearing Christian, I take seriously the words of Proverbs 13:22, which state: "A good man leaveth an inheritance to his children's children." On your way to attaining the financial freedom you'll need to become a millionaire, don't neglect to purchase life, health and disability insurance to protect your family's financial security. Why? Because life insurance will provide money to take your place in covering your family's living expenses, in the event you die prematurely or become disabled while you're pursuing your dreams. It's not impossible for things to happen that could derail your dreams. Insurance is protection that can allow your dreams to come true—no matter what happens to you.

While you are alive, you are a "money-making machine" supplying the money your loved ones need to live on. But imagine the picture for them if you're no longer alive. Would you want them to suffer financially? Of course not. So don't just think about adequately insuring your family's future, make some tangible steps today towards doing it. I'll be offering a set of steps for you to follow later in this discussion.

We've discussed the need for life insurance in the event that you die prematurely. But what if you live? Even if you don't die prematurely, if you purchase the right kind of insurance, the same policy will build cash to help take care of your retirement needs. With the money you're going to build up as an investor, and the security you'll have with the right insurance policy, the years you spend in retirement can truly be "golden."

Whether your life insurance consists of term insurance, the universal life plan, or the whole life plan, your family will benefit from the cash buildup. Let's look at the primary difference between term and whole life insurance. Term life insurance is temporary. It lasts for a specified period of time, usually anywhere from 10-30 years, or to age 99. After that time, it becomes too expensive to keep. However, the advantage of this kind of insurance is that it can meet your needs well on a shorter-term basis at the lowest cost. On the other hand, permanent life insurance—also called universal or whole life insurance—accumulates cash value within the policy on a tax-deferred basis. That means this insurance can be kept in use even if you live to be a hundred years old. So whether you live or die prematurely, with the right kind and amount of insurance, you still win. Using term insurance, you must save the money you will use in your savings plan by not buying whole life—in order to have a cash build up.

You may want to consider life insurance products that will pay living benefits if you should ever face a potentially long-term illness, such as cancer, heart attack, stroke, coronary bypass surgery, Alzheimer's disease, or a major organ transplant operation. This same policy will pay to your beneficiary the face amount of the policy upon your death.

One company we represent in Dallas has what they call a "comprehensive added protection plan." This company offers many types of plans and products, but I like this particular one, because you don't have to designate your mortgage company or any other creditor, leaving your beneficiary the option of paying the debts they desire to pay. The main point I'm making is that if something happens to the primary breadwinner, the family will have the cash they need to use as they see fit.

Every year at Century 21 Galloway-Herron, we have some client or other who is forced to sell their home because they can no longer afford the mortgage payments when a primary breadwinner dies unexpectedly. Many times, such families slip into poverty because they have made no provisions to protect themselves from such unfortunate occurrences. Many times when this happens, the surviving family members are left with no choice but to move into an apartment or back home with mom and dad. In the worst cases, there are no relatives that are able to help a family suddenly faced with poverty—a family that only a few days earlier was a home-owning middle class family. But there is no good reason for this to happen to you, or any other family. Many people might think they cannot afford life insurance, when in actuality, they can't afford to be without it. Don't let unfortunate turns of events derail your dreams of becoming financially independent. Do the things you need to do today, to make sure that your wishes will be fulfilled, whether or not you are around to see them fulfilled. A good family financial manager with a prosperity-focused millionaire mindset will do what it takes to make sure an inheritance is left for his or her family, in the event of an unexpected or untimely death. I'll state here, once again, the words of Proverbs 13:22: "A good man leaveth an inheritance to his children's children."

## Most Americans Are Underinsured. Are You?

Do you have 6-10 times your income stashed away somewhere so that your family will be cared for if something were to happen to you? Most people will have to truthfully answer "No" to this question, because it is nearly impossible to save money at the rate you'd need to save to have that much put aside when you have to work for a living. Yet that's exactly how much money many professionals believe you need to continue your same standards of living, especially if you have young children. Therefore, a person earning $75,000 per year would need to have at least $450,000 in insurance, which would be six times his or her income.

The fact is most Americans are underinsured. We don't have enough of it. To illustrate this point, let me share a little story with you. I'm told it's true, but I have my doubts. Still, it makes a good point, comically punctuating what I'm discussing in this section.

A man told me that a woman was reported to the sheriff of the county for grave robbing once. The sheriff rushed out to the cemetery and found a woman digging up a freshly covered grave. As the sheriff approached the grave she kept digging until he ordered her to stop.

"So what in the hell do you think you are doing?" asked the sheriff.

The woman of about 50 years of age was tired and she sat down on the ground to catch her breath. She said, "Sheriff, the man in this grave is my husband."

Bewildered, the sheriff asked, "Why are you digging him up? He is dead, isn't he?"

"Yes, he is dead and that's the problem," she said.

"You see sheriff, my husband told me he had $50,000 worth of insurance before he died. Therefore, I spent all my money putting him away nice. I even bought him a new suit and pocket watch with a new gold chain. I buried him in that new suit and with the pocket watch. Today the insurance man came and I found out he never had a $50,000 policy. He only had $5,000. He had not paid the premium for over a year and it had lapsed. So, Mr. Sheriff, you may as well go on because as soon as I can get my breath back I am going to finish digging up this scoundrel and get my new suit and gold watch."

The sheriff asked, "Then what will you do with him?"

She replied, "I don't care what happens to him. For leaving me like this, the buzzards can eat him for all I care!"

I have always questioned if the above story is fact or fiction. In the final analysis, whether or not it is true is not the point. The point of the story has been well made. The woman in the story was correct in thinking that today there is no excuse for leaving your family unsecured. As someone who was born and raised in the rural South, I know that many years ago poor black people did not know how to purchase protection, or companies would not allow them to purchase protection. Today any man or woman who is not prevented because of health reasons should not leave his or her family at risk. Your dreams don't have to leave this earth when you do. In fact, it should be part of your plans for your future that your dreams of financial freedom outlive you, so that your family will enjoy this freedom for generations to come because of the foundation you began in your lifetime. I truly expect no member of my family coming after me to ever be poverty-stricken, unless they choose to be.

## A "Millionaire Mindset" Protects Assets

If you truly want to use the income and assets that you accumulate as a working person to become a millionaire, you are going to have to begin to develop what I call a "millionaire mindset." This type of mindset is essential to protecting and preserving what you are able to accumulate, on the way to achieving your financial dreams. If you don't make up your mind to think like someone set on keeping and preserving, as you acquire and accumulate, your income from your job will never be enough to make you a "self-made" millionaire.

Now is the time to begin developing the mindset you will need to keep what you have long enough to build upon it. Your home is one big part of this plan.

The home is the center of life for most families. It is the place where you live your life with your spouse, start your family, raise your children, and/or enjoy your retirement years. Unfortunately, all the hard work and savings you acquire, and all that you put into the building and maintaining of your home, can quickly be put at risk upon the death, disability, or life-threatening illness of a primary breadwinner. Without the income this person provides, your most important material assets can be lost.

Thankfully, there is such a thing as insurance that offers us a way to protect what we accumulate, even if something unfortunate should happen on the way to achieving our dreams. There are insurance policies and plans that will cover life, accidents, and disability, all in one policy. This type of policy can have what is called a "return of premium" rider. Simply put, if you never use this insurance, all of your premium will be returned to you. Therefore, no breadwinner for any household should ever be without this coverage.

To understand insurance—something no one wants to think about or talk about—we have to think about it, and we have to talk about it. If you're truly developing a millionaire mindset, you will make up your mind to begin thinking differently about something so essential to maintaining and protecting your financial security. Don't allow the fear of death to scare you away from shielding what you have worked all your life to accumulate. Every one of us, one day, is going to die. None of us know if our time of departure will be sooner or later, but we all know we will not live forever. We also cannot know what state of health we might face in life before we pass away. Therefore, it is in your best interest, and that of your family, to not face the risk alone. Sure, you might have to pay a monthly premium to keep good insurance for you and your material assets. But isn't it better to do so, and to shift the financial risk to a big insurance company, with deep pockets?

## How Well Are You Managing Life's Inescapable "Risks"?

The need for insurance is linked to our need to manage risk. Your developing millionaire mindset should be alert already about the need to manage or minimize any risk associated with living and with losing what you are working for.

There is always risk associated with something of value. Our lives are valuable, and even more so to a spouse and children. Hence, the need for life insurance. Also, the plan for financial freedom you're going to begin building after reading this book is going to be something of great value. Therefore, there is a need to manage the risk associated with this value.

In many households where there are two working parents, the risk is that one or both of them may not, for whatever reason, be able to continue contributing to the financial health of the household. While the investments you're going to make, and the business you're going to build will help ease the financial burden for your family, you're still in need of the added protection of insurance. In fact, as you accumulate more wealth, it becomes even more vital that you manage the risks associated with living. For this reason, there are two major types of insurance that are absolutely required: life insurance and health insurance. Life insurance is required in the event you die prematurely. Health insurance is needed in case of sickness or disability.

Health insurance has obvious benefits for the financial well being of your family if you should become sick or disabled. All insurance, health and life, should be purchased as early as possible because the older you get, the more costly insurance is going to be. You should speak with a knowledgeable insurance professional to check up on your coverage, making sure you have the plans right for you. What's right for a one person may not be right for another person. For example, a single person will most likely need a different plan from one designed for a married couple with no children, or for a family where there are young children.

You may be among the many Americans who get group health insurance through their jobs. Or, you could be covered through a family member's insurance at work. This type of coverage is usually the least expensive kind, and the employer pays all or a portion of the cost.

From time to time, you should check your insurance coverage, to make sure it still meets your needs. As your family grows, or as you purchase a more expensive home, acquiring increased income or increased debt, your needs for coverage will change. You will need to upgrade your insurance policies to reflect these changes so that you're adequately covered. You need to make sure you will have enough money to pay for your medical and living expenses in the event your income from your job is lost. You should have disability and critical illness coverage to manage the risk that could result from losing your earning power if for some reason you or your spouse became unable to work.

Checking up on your coverage is something you're going to need to do periodically. Keep your plans in harmony with your life. As things change for you and/or your family, adjustments may be needed in your coverage. Keep paying the premium as long as you have income to do so. Never forget that this is an important step as you move your family toward financial security.

## What About Insurance For Your Business?

If you decide to start a business, there are several kinds of insurance that you are going to need to obtain. Here is an overview of the three major types of coverage you'll need:

1. **Property Insurance.** To protect your business's assets, you're going to need property insurance—in the same manner that you need homeowner's insurance to protect your home. Any assets you own

that you decide to transfer to your business entity should be covered by your business property insurance policies.

2. **Workers' Compensation.** If you become an employer, you will be required to obtain this insurance from a private insurance company. Most states require employers to have workers compensation, by law. This type of insurance pays benefits to employees who suffer job- related injuries.

4. **Liability Insurance.** Businesses need appropriate and adequate liability insurance to cover work-related risks. It doesn't matter if your business entity is a "limited liability" concern. You will still need liability insurance.

Some things are better to have and not need, than to need and not have. Access to a good attorney is one of these things. As you pave your path to greater financial freedom, you need to understand that the more you own, and the more business-related ventures you become involved with, the greater will be your need to manage legal risks that can sometimes come with the territory, or crop up unexpectedly.

Everyone needs the services of an attorney at one time or another. You want to make sure that if something happens to you, that you have a will in place so that your family will know how you want your assets divided in the event of your death. Or you might have a need for advice about a tax matter.

## *Summary of Step 7*
## Make Sure You Have Good Insurance

Insurance is the way you are going to protect your dream. And while I hope and pray that God will grant you long life, if He decides to call you home before all your earthly dreams are realized, you should make sure your family will get a chance to enjoy what you have been working to achieve. Protecting your dream will also help you enjoy more financial freedom while you are living and breathing. Insurance has many functions, and many possibilities. Developing a positive and proactive attitude about insurance is part of the "millionaire mindset".

# Invest and Make Your
# Money Work for You

8

How do you make money grow? There's no such thing as a "money tree," so we know money does not grow the way leaves grow on a tree. Most of us learned this important lesson about money as young children when our mothers informed us early and often that "Money doesn't grow on trees." However, the lesson of my last statement not withstanding, money does indeed grow on trees, if you own the forest.

As adults scrounging around in the work-a-day world, we soon realize the importance of our mother's wisdom. In fact, it becomes increasingly apparent as we watch our paychecks slip through our hands every month, like leaves scurrying away on the wind, that dollars are much harder to rake up than leaves.

So how does money grow? The answer to this question should be of great interest to anyone desiring to enjoy sustained financial freedom.

Through the years, some people have had some interesting notions about ways to make their money multiply, quickly. Winning the lottery, for example, is a popular notion. Every week, millions and millions of Americans invest $1, $3, $5, or even more dollars into the state-run lottery jackpot. Unfortunately for most them, gambling does not pay off. Instead of doubling or tripling their money, most of these anxious gamblers end up with a few dollars less than they had in the beginning.

Then, there are those people we keep hearing about on the six o'clock news, who keep handing their money over to schemers promising outrageous returns on their investment. It's always the same: a regular, every-day working or retired man or woman, seemingly of at least average intelligence, is standing in front of a news announcer's microphone relating a story about how they met someone who looked and seemed so trustworthy.

This familiar story always goes on to tell us how the *victims* gave the schemer all or a large sum of their hard-earned money, which the schemer promised to "invest" in one thing or another. An investment, according to the schemer, that would surely double or triple the *victim's* money in a matter of months (or in even less time!) However, as the story always ends, a few months later the schemer has absconded with all the cash. Now the "victim/investor" knows, for real, why the opportunity sounded "too good to be true."

There may actually be shortcuts to making your money grow. There may actually be "get rich quick" schemes and operations that really do work, but I have to tell you, I have not found them. And I spend a lot of time looking for ways to grow my money. The main point I'm making here—the bottom line—is that you should put your money into more tried-and-true investment alternatives.

I believe you should stay away from things that cannot possibly be the best ways for you to expect your money to multiply. That doesn't mean you should never buy another lottery ticket. It does mean, however, that you should not be spending a lot of your hard-earned money on lottery tickets. If you must play, one or two dollars a month should be all you invest in it. (I'm not endorsing playing the lottery, but I believe if you're going to win it, it will happen even if you purchase only one ticket a year!) But if you're spending $20 a week on lottery tickets, that's $80 a month you could be investing into mutual funds, or some other kind of investment program guaranteed to pay off for you.

It's best to face the brutal truth that "get rich quick" scenarios don't work out for most people. Usually, the only people seeing a return from them are those offering the propositions. And while money can be grown in many different ways, for most of us, all of these ways take time. The sooner you and I accept this truth, the sooner we can begin seeking out and finding ways of investing our money offering us greater probabilities of a return. Frankly, even state-run lotteries take advantage of poor people's dreams of making it rich, with odds that are greater than 36 million to one. This is not a sound way to make money. It's not God's way. As a businessman, and as a God-fearing person, I cannot endorse the lottery. I think it should be banned because they take advantage of the poor.

## Good and Sound Ways to Grow Money

While growing your money is most likely not going to happen quickly, it is also not going to happen by leaving it alone. I'm sure you've heard of people saving money under mattresses because they don't trust banks. They erroneously think that when they decide to retrieve it, they will have at least exactly the amount they placed under the mattress in the first place. Wrong! Money either increases or it shrinks. It does not maintain its present value forever. A dollar tucked under the mattress today, in 10 years, will have lost value due to inflation and increases in the cost of living.

Knowing this, we should look then to increasing the value of our dollars by investing where money can earn interest or a return. There are numerous ways to accomplish this. However, until you become sophisticated in making other kinds of investments, I would recommend you put your money into an interest-earning account. Be aware however, that many times, the interest you earn at a bank will not outpace inflation. So as soon as you have generated enough money, you will need to look for other ways to invest your money.

I realize that there is a multitude of vehicles in which to invest, but I am going to confine my discussion to real estate. After all, I am a successful real estate professional, and most of my investment success has come directly from real estate. Also, I know that real estate still represents one of the most "sound" of all kinds of investments, and I know what it will do for you. For the most part, real estate is always going to appreciate in value. There may be times in the short run that real estate values will go down, but in the long run, it will go up.

Confining my discussion to real estate, therefore, is still going to provide you with a variety of creative investment options. That's because there are many ways to invest in it. One thing you can do, for example, is to invest in single-family homes. This is an uncomplicated, fairly easy investment option for the first-time investor to master. That's because it doesn't require a great deal of knowledge or advanced study. Anyone who can purchase a home (and that's virtually anyone) can become an investor in real estate. Once you become more sophisticated about investing, you can begin to explore opportunities in commercial real estate. With the right help, you can invest in almost any property. Real estate brokers can assist you.

Once you get the hang of investing, your investments can work harder for you, creating the most success for you. For example, that money you invested in the bank earns money whether it's raining or snowing at night or all day. Your real estate investments from which you receive rent and appreciation earn revenue every month and increase in value, except in times of deflation. (Don't be alarmed. Over the last 40 years we've had only a few pockets of deflation.)

Let me assure you that ownership of real estate will move you toward financial security. Because of inflation and something known as "leverage," real estate gives you the multiplier effect. It means you can take $10,000 and control $100,000 worth of property. Or better still, you can take $100,000 and control $1,000,000 worth of property. Therefore, inflation causes the value of real estate to increase, while leverage allows you to gain property valued at $1,000,000, when you put in only $100,000 of your money.

Let's take a closer look at the concepts of inflation and leverage. For the sake of this example, let us assume that inflation is around 5% each year. If you were able to purchase $100,000 worth of property with your own money, because of inflation, you would have a gain of $5,000. On the other hand, if you used leverage, making a down payment of $100,000 and borrowing $900,000 to purchase a $1,000,000 property, the same 5% inflation rate would give you a gain of $50,000. That's because the use of Other People's Money (OPM) to increase your wealth is truly a great thing. However, if overused or unwisely used, it can destroy you financially faster than it can build wealth.

If you want to speed up your timetable toward financial security, then investing more to gain more is a most important step. By using this step, you can speed up the day that you become financially independent. Therefore, your financial independence is dependent only on the methods you use, and the assets you acquire.

There are numerous stories told about some individuals saving their money for 10, 15, and 20 years and losing it to some grand scheme perpetuated by some unscrupulous person, or even some well-meaning individual. As illustrated by the story I told in the beginning of this chapter, there are people who will risk their life savings on a promise (or a scheme) to multiply investments to a point that guarantees almost "instant" wealth. But let me say—clearly—you should never invest in a highly suspect venture, or with an individual or institution with no track record of being successful in the kinds of investments they're proposing for you. If someone approaches you, and you are in doubt about their track record, you should seek professional advice about the investment opportunity from people with the proper credentials.

More small fortunes are lost as the result of people putting money into unsound investments promising "chance of a lifetime returns."

Why do we keep falling prey to such promises time and time again? I believe we do it because human nature contains a healthy dose of greed, and—if unchecked—it's easy for someone to convince us that he or she can take our $10,000 and easily turn it into 10 times, or 15 times what it is worth. Therefore, it is important to recognize that we can fall prey to greed. Acknowledging this fact can save you. Because if you know you have a tendency to give in to the siren call of greed, you are in a better position to keep greed in check. Denial of this fact can allow your guards to come down.

If you are not careful to keep greed in check, in the process of trying to gain more money too quickly, you can lose all you've saved, and all you've managed to gain up to this point. If you fall prey to a bad investment offer, not only will you not benefit from the interest or income from your principal, but also allowing yourself to be guided by greed—rather than by good common sense—can cause you to lose your principal as well. If that happens, you could be faced with having to start over with few or no working years remaining. Once your assets are lost, starting over can be traumatic and personally painful, not to mention the economic and physical difficulties you could face.

## What Makes Real Estate Such an Attractive Investment?

The primary reason to invest in real estate is the potential for high returns on your investment. Real estate offers investors a way to diversify their holdings in terms of the kinds of properties purchased, as well as in the property locations and economic areas invested in. There are several other very good reasons you should consider investing in real estate as a way to grow your money on your way to greater financial freedom:

1. **Equity.** As you pay for your investment property, you're continually building up equity (which you can then borrow against to make more investments). The shorter your loan period, the faster you will gain more equity in your investment.

2. **Cash Flow.** Investing in real estate can allow you to spend money, and still have cash flow. It's true. Whether you invest in single- or multi-family housing, it is possible for you to have money left after paying your expenses. In fact, this is the main reason banks will lend you money to purchase real estate—the possibility of your being able to earn money, regularly, on your investment.

3. **Value Appreciation.** Real estate is likely to appreciate in value. How do I know that? One way I know is because the home I purchased 20 years ago is worth more today than it was when I bought it. The truth is, just about any home purchased many years ago, if it has been maintained well, is likely to be worth a good percentage more today than when it was purchased. That's because, typically, real estate appreciates in value. Whether we are discussing land or homes, real estate values increase, typically.

4. **Need.** The need for real estate is continuing to grow, because the U.S. and the world population is growing steadily. And, it is likely to continue growing steadily in the future. Therefore, more people living in the country, through the birthrate or through immigration, means more need for housing. Do the math. It's really a very simple formula. Investing in housing is a smart, common sense thing to do. The lessons taught in elementary economics courses state that if the supply is fixed (land) and the demand increases (people), the price will go up.

## Single-Family Homes as Investments

The single-family home is still one of the very best investments available to an individual in America.

I know that the value of homes, from time to time, may drop in some areas of the country—mostly in the short-run. There are definitely some areas in the United States where we've experienced declines in property values over the short term. This is mainly due to business cycles that are traditional. But in spite of these factors, I reiterate my statement that the single-family home is still one of the best investments an individual can make.

Why is this so?

First of all, fast-growing metropolitan areas, such as Dallas, Ft. Worth, Houston, and some areas in Florida and California are experiencing a tremendous population growth, and therefore, greater appreciation in the value of property. Let's look at why, in the long run, these property values must continue to go up.

First, realize there is only so much land available. As the population continues to grow, no new land is being produced. So, it is basic elementary economics involving the principle of supply and demand. When you have a fixed supply of something, and the demand for it increases, then the price has to increase. It cannot remain at one level.

With no more land being created, and with constant increases in the population, there will continue to be increasing demand on our fixed supply of land. As a result, even if the cost of production of building a home remained the same, the land cost alone would increase the value of the home. Unfortunately, the cost of production will not remain the same because of increasing labor costs, and increases in all the other materials required to build a home. Consequently, the value of a single-family home will increase automatically. That means if you buy single-family homes as investments, the odds are great that you're going to have an increase in value over time. If the homes you purchase increase in value, then you're going to increase your net worth. In the long run, the only question to ask is how fast the increase will occur.

Another reason to invest in single-family homes is for income purposes. There will always be people who, for some reason, will prefer to rent rather than purchase a home. Perhaps they think they cannot afford to buy. Still, they must live somewhere. These people will be your tenants, thus creating income for you.

Of course, in the early stages of your investment career, if you use maximum leverage, your principal benefit may be the tax advantage provided by a home. The revenue from the property minus its expenses may leave you a positive cash flow, or you could break even. When you add the depreciation, however, you could show a loss. That loss is deducted from your income tax, based on your particular tax bracket, thus decreasing your tax liability.

In later years, your loan value will decrease and your equity will build, but your mortgage payment will remain stable if you have a fixed-rate loan. If you are renting, however, your rent will increase. Therefore, ownership can result in a positive cash flow in income to you over the life of your property. By the time you're ready to retire (in 20 years or so), your home should be debt free. If you've set up your mortgage payments well, it should then be yours—lock, stock, and barrel. In this instance, you would have all the income from the property, less expenses, for retirement income.

Let's now do a brief recap of what I've talked to you about in this section. I've talked about investing in single-family homes for these four primary reasons:

1. Increasing your net worth
2. Increasing your tax advantages while you are still working
3. Having additional sources of income
4. Retirement income

The previously mentioned list comprises the four primary reasons you should now begin considering investing in single-family homes. Such property is not hard to purchase, and the more you buy, the more financial security you're gathering for your future.

Most of the investors to whom I have sold property have called me up wanting to buy more. Not once have I had an investor who did not want to own additional properties. That's proof to me that once people understand investing, and start to invest in properties, they see the benefits and all of the advantages. When it dawns on them that they have discovered a really good thing, they want to keep doing it. Historically speaking, at least since the Great Depression, the single-family home has out-performed any other type of investment.

Let us now stretch our imaginations a bit. While discussing purchasing just one property for investment, let us make some predictions for the next 20 years. Consider that today you may be earning $400 a month on an investment property. If that investment income triples over 20 years, you will be receiving $1200 a month on that one property. That's income of $14,400 a year. This should make it clear to you how you can increase your wealth, your net worth, your income, and your ability to retire and not sit in the rocking chair worrying and waiting from one Social Security check to the next. Instead, picture yourself on the beaches of Hawaii and other exotic places with all your investment income coming in. Isn't that a much nicer vision for your future? And all it takes for you to make this vision a reality is to learn some simple procedures you'll need to know to begin buying your first property. How do you do it?

Before buying that first investment property, I suggest you have your home and life insurance in place, so that in the event you die prematurely, your family can still accomplish the goals and objectives you've set.

## A "Mini-Course" in Purchasing Investment Property

*Lesson 1:* *Find a good real estate agent for purchasing investment property.*

Your first step in the actual buying process is going to be finding a good real estate agent. You're going to need to tell that agent what you are trying to accomplish, so that he or she can locate the type of properties you desire. Throughout the buying process, you will be working with this agent. In order to select an agent, I suggest you look for one who has a positive mental attitude, who is productive, has shown stability, and has been in the business for a good amount of time. How would you find out the type of producer he is? You ask. It is perfectly all right to ask an agent what his production is. There is no magical number for this. What's important is that he has been producing on a consistent basis. He or she should also have knowledge about the particular area/locations where you want to buy your property, because that means he knows the property values.

Does this mean you should never work with an agent new to real estate? Not necessarily. Sometimes, new and inexperienced agents with the proper attitude can provide excellent service, because this person will most likely make every effort to please you. I have changed my mind over the many years that I have been in the real estate business about using experienced agents versus new agents. I am now of the belief that if a new agent is working for a company with a reputation for high productivity—such as Century 21 Galloway-Herron—or another good company, these new agents may be better able to help you than many of the experienced agents that have been in business for a long time, but who are not very productive.

At Century 21 Galloway-Herron, the new agents are in training for the first six months, and they always have access to a team of managers and other support people in the office. Also, they may have "new energy" and will be eager to get the job done to your satisfaction.

Once you select a real estate agent, a lot of your work will be eliminated. You will have a knowledgeable professional working for you. He or she will look for property you can buy for 90% or less of market value. Then, with good enough credit, you can get the entire 90% financed.

*Lesson 2: Plan on holding on to your cash (your liquidity), putting as little money into a property as possible.*

I firmly believe you should put as little money as possible into a property. By keeping as much of your cash as you can in your bank account, you'll be able to take advantage of other investment or business opportunities. With this in mind, you should try to buy your first investment property for nothing down, if possible. If that's not possible, then you will probably pay from a small percentage down all the way up to 20%.

You should not refuse to buy a property because you have to pay a significant amount down, but you should still try to buy it for the smallest possible amount of money down. Most lenders require an investor to have about 20% invested in the property. Some will allow 10%.

*Lesson 3: Where to buy?*

I suggest you buy properties in the city where you reside, and preferably close to where you actually live. I would not want to invest in a single-family home much further than a 15-minute drive from my home. The investment is so small; it is not cost effective to travel too far to oversee one single-family home. If it were an apartment complex, or a shopping center, or some similar potentially high-income-generating property, the distance would not matter. If you lived in San Francisco, and the property was in New York, if the income is large enough to justify the travel, then it is worth the trip.

That's the end of your "mini-course." Now you are ready for a little test. Let's say you have found a property with an appraised value of $120,000, and you are able to purchase it for $108,000—which is 90% of the appraised value. The property has an assumable outstanding loan in the amount of $88,000. If you have $20,000 to pay down, you may assume the $88,000 loan and acquire the property that way. On the other hand, what if you have only $10,000 to pay down? *Question*: What could you do to still acquire that property?

*Answer*: You could get the seller to carry back a second lien in the amount of $10,000. Then, you would also assume the original loan in the amount of $88,000. You have now purchased the property for $108,000. That is, you paid $10,000 down, got a second lien for $10,000, and assumed the $88,000 loan.

Let's have a little more fun with this. Let's go and refinance the property we just acquired. Remember, the appraised value of the property is $120,000. Now that you own the property, the purchase price has no bearing on the amount of the loan.

Therefore, you might go to the bank and get a 90% loan to refinance the property. Let's say you have a 700 credit score, which is very good credit. This will allow you to get a 90% loan to value on the property. The following table demonstrates what you should do with the loan:

## The Loan and Use of Funds

| | |
|---|---|
| Appraised Value | $120,000 |
| Loan at 90% of Value | $108,000 |
| Pay off First Lien | $88,000 |
| Pay off Second Lien | $10,000 |
| Pay Back Investor's Down Payment | $10,000 |
| Total Use of Funds | $108,000 |

Now the investor (you, in this fictitious scenario) has purchased a property with $10,000 in equity and with all the cash you used for the down payment returned to your bank account. Now, I recommend that you go home and find your favorite place where you like to talk with your Creator, and say a big, heartfelt, "Thank You, Dear Lord." You've just earned $12,000; now go and pay your tithe.

## Where Does a First-Time Investor Get Money for Down Payments?

Most of the time when you purchase property, you are going to have to pay money down. Now that you've decided to be a real estate investor, where will you get the money you need to make down payments on properties? As a beginning investor, you will have a difficult time trying to follow the scenario we just went through with no money to pay down. How then do you get started?

First of all, there are not a lot of people who don't have at least a few goods and assets that can be used to raise funds. You might have an old car sitting around that's not being driven, or you might have some valuable jewelry. Anything legal you can think of that will bring you money is something you can put into purchasing your first property. The proceeds from the sale of these goods or assets can help you finance the down payment on your first property. Those of you now living in a home you bought five, six, or 20 years ago can borrow your equity out of it, and then put the money into another house.

It's true. If you own a $100,000 home, on which you owe only a $50,000 mortgage, all you have to do is ask the lender to give you a second lien mortgage for $20,000 on your property. Take that $20,000 and pay down on an investment piece of property.

First-time buyers beware of negative cash flow. I don't like negative cash flow. I make my deals based upon the fact that I'm going to break even or have a positive cash flow. When you break even, that means once you pay all bills related to your new property, what you pay out will be equal to what you take in (as income from renting your property). If your cash flow is positive, that means you should take in more than you have to pay out. On the other hand, negative cash flow is what happens when you are paying out more than you are taking in.

I refuse to buy property that doesn't provide either break-even or positive cash flow. Now there's nothing wrong with negative cash flow for those people who have enough income from other sources to offset it. But for investors who don't have a lot of other sources of income, it's best to keep cash flow positive, or even. Remember this lesson when you are making decisions about purchasing properties.

### Graduation from my "mini-course"

Now I want you to stand up and go to the mirror. What you are now looking at is an investor with a millionaire mind set. Tell yourself that you are now on your way toward the *real American dream*. Now start thinking (and making notes) about property you want to own. Develop a plan, and start making tangible steps towards making your dreams come true.

## Owning a Business: Another Way to Invest

The American dream is really not a singular dream. It is plural. Home ownership, for example, is definitely the first dream of most Americans. But coming in a strong second is the dream of owning a business.

While much of this book concerns real estate (because that is my background), I have made money in the real estate *business*. I own my own business, and therefore I have taken the American dream one step further. Because I have been very successful in the real estate business, I strongly recommend owning your own business as one of the investment options open to you on the road to gaining the financial freedom you need to become a millionaire.

If you want to own your own business, let me caution you to select one you know something about; one you will like. Why? Because you will perform a lot better as a businessperson if you are doing something you are knowledgeable about, and that you actually enjoy. You'll wake up every morning feeling thankful for the opportunity to get to run your business another day. And during the day—if you're truly cut out for the type of business you choose, you will forget you're at work. Instead, you'll just feel as though you're spending your day doing something you love very much. This, my friends is one of the best aspects of my plan for helping you realize your dream of becoming a millionaire.

**Step One:** *Getting Started*

Your first step should be to do research to find out as much information as you can about the type of business you're interested in. Find out how successful others are who are in your particular type of business. Go online as well as to the library to research the market and the market potential for your business. One of the best things you can do is find people who are in the same type of business you're proposing, and talk to them about starting a similar business, and the prospects for a good return. Some may be unwilling to talk with you (after all, you could one day be competition for them), but keep trying until you find those willing to discuss it with you.

Once you're satisfied you can make money doing what you love, you will need a business plan. I would suggest that when you prepare one, however, it is not necessary to have a fancy business plan. A simple business plan is all that is required. In fact, some of the fancy computer printouts showing pro formas (estimations or projections of what may occur in the future based on actions undertaken in the present) are sometimes not worth the paper they are printed on. In fact, some are absolutely worthless. But if the data you use in your decision-making is based on factual information—for example, if you talk with a businessperson in a similar location as the one you want to set up, and in the same business you want to go into, this might be enough information for you to proceed with your plans. In fact, there is a chance that this kind of information may be more reliable than scientifically-derived estimations or projections.

Of course, there are statistics that are published in the library and in journals that will tell you what might be the performance (or potential for success) for a particular kind of business. If the business is a franchise operation, for example, there will be information that is readily available concerning what to expect from that business.

**Step Two:** *Financing Your Business*

After deciding on your type of business, and after doing the prerequisite research, next you will determine how much money you will need to capitalize the business. Your capitalization figures should include enough money to carry your business for a year (with little or no profit). There are very few businesses where you can expect to start making a profit right away. Most of the time, you should look to have enough starting capital to pay salaries—including your salary for a year. Depending on the business, the lead-time before you turn a profit could be longer, or shorter, but you should definitely have some seed money to cover at least a one-year-long start-up period. For some businesses, you may need only 90 days.

Remember when I said earlier that you should undertake a business about which you are knowledgeable? I said that because I thought it would be logical and reasonable that you might want to start a business in the area or field you are now working in. Starting a business in what you know about can offer you "built-in" advantages, saving you both time and money. But you may be interested in something completely different from what you now know. If so, just remember that starting a business in an unfamiliar area is going to be more costly. For example, if your experience is in the pizza business and you decide that you are going to start a business in retail shoe sales, you are going to need to hire somebody already in that business. While this will be an excellent way to get the experience you need, you are going to have to pay for getting that experience.

A good place to start looking for financing alternatives is to take advantage of the various government programs offering low rates of interest. Even though these programs can be slow and cumbersome, sometimes they offer an excellent opportunity for the businessperson. Generally, you are able to get a larger loan with a government loan from the Small Business Administration than you might be able to get through a bank with no government backing or guarantee. Therefore, it is definitely advisable to look at any available government programs and take advantage of them. The web site sba.gov has links to information about financing a small business through the SBA. It can get you started on the process of getting approved for an SBA loan.

As I've stated before in this chapter, you're going to need a good business plan to help you get started. There are millions of examples of business plans out there. The SBA Web site also provides a very good sample business plan. However, what follows is a simple plan that includes what I believe to be the most important factors to be considered by anyone thinking about starting a business:

## SAMPLE BUSINESS PLAN

### 1. Business Description
   A. Business Name
   B. Location
   C. Product/Service
   D. A Mission Statement
### 2. Market Analysis
   A. Size of market served?
   B. Advantages and disadvantages of product/service?
   C. Who is my customer?
   D. Who is my competition?

### 3. Marketing Plan
   A. How will product/service be priced?
   B. What makes product/service different from other businesses?
   C. How will product/service be advertised and promoted?
   D. How will product/service be distributed?

### 4. Management Plan
   A. How will the business be organized?
   B. How many people will be employed?
   C. Do key people have expertise in product/ service?

### 5. Financial Plan (Monthly for three years)
   A. Business expenses
   B. Sales revenue
   C. Break Even Point—When will sales match expenses?

## A Special Message for African-Americans

From 1982 to 1985, I spent three years as president of the Dallas Black Chamber of Commerce. It was a phenomenal experience for me that really opened my eyes. Rather than teaching me a lot of new things, the experience confirmed my belief that in order for members of minority communities to get ahead, more need to consider owning businesses.

There is still a greater chance for more people to become wealthy through owning a business and employing other people than there is for winning the lottery. Therefore, more people from minority populations—especially African-Americans—need to begin thinking about practical ways to make money, and I don't see anything more practical than owning your own business. Just as with home ownership, business ownership helps you build equity in something of your own, for yourself and your family, instead of only using your money to help others enjoy the fruits of ownership.

This new Millennium has brought us to a time when we're seeing blacks performing at the top of the business spectrum like never before. We're now making it inside and beyond the sports arenas. American Express's CEO (as of the time of the writing of this book) is an African-American. Oprah Winfrey is the world's first black American billionaire. Black musicians continue to top the charts as sellers of their talent—and now, their business skills. No longer should any person from a minority group feel their race—alone—is the thing that is holding them back from accomplishing their financial dreams. Although race may play a role, I don't believe it is the major battle any more. It can be used as an excuse, but it is not a valid reason anymore for lack of trying. Rather, the battle we should be focusing our time and attention on is for knowledge, information, courage, preparedness, common sense, assertiveness, aggressiveness, perseverance, and unwillingness to give up. These are the things we must cultivate and/or attain now in order to be successful. We have to believe in ourselves first and foremost. That is key. Once we are able to do this, we are then ready to work towards the rest (which is easy compared to learning how to believe in yourself, always).

I hope it is obvious to everyone by now that we cannot (and should not) depend on any of the governmental entities for our salvation—whether federal, state, or local. Of course, we need (and as citizens are entitled to) the help of these entities, but we must begin our ultimate journey to self-sufficiency in our own neighborhoods. The entrepreneurial spirit is what sparked the building of America, and I believe entrepreneurs will build our communities to greatness, taking them out of a poverty-stricken state.

And that's not all. Entrepreneurs will accomplish some other things too. First of all, many people who create the businesses and become successful are going to become wealthy. They are going to provide jobs for other people. Also, in that same area where businesses are located, the property will become more valuable. So the entrepreneurial spirit is a rising tide that lifts all boats.

I wrote 20 years ago that the truth of the matter is that some of the neighborhoods and areas of our American cities are similar to an undeveloped country. This, unfortunately, is still true today. It is also still true, as it was 20 years ago, that the great majority of people owning the businesses in African-American neighborhoods are from other ethnic and racial groups. I have no problem with these other people owning businesses and operating them in our neighborhoods, or anywhere else for that matter. That's the American free enterprise system at work. But I would still like to see more African-Americans owning more businesses in communities where blacks outnumber other racial or ethnic groups. We must own more businesses in and beyond our own communities. It's still the only way we will be able to exert more control over our collective future. Of course, I recommend ownership of businesses all over town, and in any state.

There is only one way greater numbers of African-Americans are going to become financially independent. We are going to have to do it ourselves. The sooner we accept that nobody else is going to do it for us, the sooner we can start the process of self-help. We must start teaching our children in the same fashion that we instruct them in Biblical principles. Just as we teach them "Our Father which art in Heaven," we must also teach them the way of entrepreneurship. The idea of owning their business must be so imbedded in them that they know it like they know the Lord's Prayer. Remember, Jesus Christ was a carpenter by trade. He was in business for Himself.

I hope we have come a long way towards creating a new mindset in our communities. I hope we're on our way to raising a generation of people who, instead of thinking "Where can I get a job," will think instead, "How can I create my own job?" With a "create-my-own-job" mindset, we will have a generation of people becoming financially independent and more influential for generations to come.

Entrepreneurship is very important for wealth creation, job creation, and family stability. We live in a democratic society, and in most cases, the people who have the money will get elected to public offices. Controlling our financial destiny, therefore, is key to controlling our political destiny. We have to get into all aspects of self-governance. We cannot sit by idly and allow others to control our destiny. No matter how much progress we have made as a people in the last half of the 20th Century, we must live in this new Millennium as if we are still involved in an important struggle, because we are. The stakes are high, and we—as owners of businesses—will have a chance to prosper and become wealthy. As business owners, we will employ other people, and will no longer have to always be worried about being the last hired and the first fired. Today, there is no plausible reason for any of us to feel we cannot do these things. Today, no matter what is your racial or ethnic background, you live in a time when all things are possible. Believe that, and believe in yourself, and you can do just about anything you set your mind to!

It is absolutely essential that we do this. We must not continue to fall prey to "self-inflicted" brainwashing. What I mean is, don't believe the fallacy passed down from days of old that said it is not possible for blacks to run successful, professional, high-quality businesses. Don't believe something that can only serve to hinder you, if you're black. I've seen evidence of acceptance of this fallacy among people in all sorts of professions: Lawyers, doctors, real estate people, even preachers! I have met people working in all these areas who truly believe that African-American people cannot perform successfully in a business venture.

Let me go on record here as saying that any black person who thinks that way must not think very much of himself or herself. If any African-American thinks they have to go to a proprietor of a different race in order to get competent service, then they most likely believe, subconsciously, in their own inferiority. Surely if they believed in their own competence, they could also believe it's possible for other African-Americans to also be competent. We should give each other the same opportunity to serve us that we give to people of other racial groups. Sure there are some of us who are not competent, and who don't run businesses in a professional manner. There are incompetent people from all racial and ethnic groups running businesses in America. We are no different. Some of us are capable, competent professionals, and others of us are not. But we should not paint everyone with the same brush. Some of us are the quintessential professionals, and there are top quality black professionals in all work categories. So open up your mind and give us a break and a try.

Any thinking individual should know that financial independence and wealth are created through determination and hard work backed by a disciplined commitment to follow a plan. And the beauty of this formula is that it will work for anyone—without regard to race, sex, creed, religion or national origin. If you think you can do it, you can. As Dr. Martin Luther King, Jr. said "It's not the color of your skin that counts but the content of your character." Just say, "Yes I can," mean it, and do it.

With the commitment to starting more businesses in our own communities comes the need to start shopping and buying in our own communities. After all, if you want people to buy from you, you must be willing to spend money in their neighborhood. It's a give and take situation. This kind of giving can establish the foundation we need to change our communities into the great living oases they can all become. All we have to do is start spending more dollars in areas populated by blacks. If we start spending money in these neighborhoods, we will be providing the groundwork for revolutionizing them.

The next revolution in America will be the continued economic revitalization of the inner city. What is occurring now in many of our neighborhoods represents a total trade imbalance. First of all, we have a disproportionate (smaller) share of the money coming into our communities. That is number one. We are not receiving a fair share of income dollars. Then we take that disproportionately small amount—which we get in a paycheck—and take it right back out of our communities by giving it to the man across town. And that is economic nonsense.

We should start to own more businesses, and we should spend for food, clothing, gasoline, etc. in our neighborhoods, as much as we possibly can. And if the fancy stores with the prestigious labels and ridiculous prices want our business, let them build in our neighborhoods. Anyone who thinks he has to have something from a particular store has been brainwashed. Advertising is a very powerful thing, and it exists to change your mind about products and services. But you cannot be a slave to advertising. You must learn to be more in control of what you allow yourself to believe. Don't be guilty of being at the mercy of the next sensational advertising campaign. Think for yourself. Make good buying decisions that are in your best interest.

The three years I spent at the Dallas Black Chamber of Commerce, and more than 30 years in the real estate industry have placed me in positions to know a lot of people. Most of us don't know the people in our neighborhoods who have the money.

A lot of us think the people that have the money are those driving around in the Mercedes and Hummers. But most of the time, those are just the people who are spending their money as fast as it comes in. And many of them are living from paycheck to paycheck. No, the people who have the money are those who own and operate the service stations, barbecue restaurants, and other fast-food businesses. A lot of the people we see working for major corporations and driving expensive automobiles don't really have any money. They have above-average cash flow coming in, but they also have above-average expenses. Their money is leaving their hands, just as fast as it comes in—or faster. It is the business people who have money, and who have the potential for making more money, because—in many ways—they have more control over their own finances. And that's what more of us need to be focusing on, instead of always looking for our next job working for someone else.

I believe significant progress has been made in educating a lot of blacks about the value of business ownership. However, more work still needs to be done. Basically, we have three segments of people in our society that can get this message across so that we can continue working to achieve the goal of widespread business ownership in the black communities across the nation. These three segments include:

- **K-12 Schools.** This is how we reach and teach our children. We need to become more involved in our PTAs, making sure our children's curricula include classes designed to teach them about business ownership. Even children's play activities can be used to teach them business principles. And it's never too early to start. First, we must get more involved in going into our schools, helping teach the children the mindset of business ownership. The schools are always looking for people to come in and talk to the children. All we have to do is tell them we are available. We need to get the message to all children in all our schools, promoting the idea of becoming entrepreneurs and owners of businesses. They need to know about business ownership as an option for their lives and livelihoods, even before they go to college. By the time they enter college, it's often too late for them to develop the "ownership" mindset, because many of them will have developed the mindset of getting a degree so that they can go work for a corporation. Getting a degree is good, but getting a degree and starting a business is even better.

- **The Church.** A lot of our larger churches are now getting more involved in education and in the building of communities, taking care of people's physical needs, as well as their spiritual needs. I commend these efforts and hope to see more church bodies across the nation becoming even more involved in community-building activities. I want to see more Churches "walking their talk" in their own neighborhoods. I'm not downplaying the notion that it is of paramount importance for people to develop their spiritual souls for the hereafter. That's important. But we also have to consider our physical needs while we are living in our physical bodies. Even Christ ministered to people's physical needs, so that He could have their attention in order to minister to their spiritual needs. He fed the multitudes so that they would be able to be filled with the Holy Spirit, without having to suppress hunger pains. Therefore, it is important for churches to be devoted to helping people improve their physical lives and physical well-being, as well as attending to people's spiritual needs.

- **The Existing Business Community.** Many members of the existing business community are already headed in the right direction, creating jobs, enhancing buying power, opening up economic opportunities, and leading community leadership and uplift. This segment is the third prong of my three-pronged attack to encourage increased business ownership or entrepreneurship.

In summary, some of the main reasons more African-Americans do not own businesses are: the lack of capital, the lack of a sufficient number of role models, and the fact that too many of us do not have the right mindset about business ownership. We grow up and get trained to work for others, whereas in other communities, people grow up and are trained to anticipate that they are going to be owners of businesses. Blacks need to begin instilling this type of mentality early on in our children's lives. That is the way to make sure that future generations will pass down this important value.

One thing is certain: we are not afraid of hard work. So the fact that owning a business demands long hours of work should have no bearing on our being business owners. Looking back at history, you can see that we are some of the hardest-working people in the history of the world. In fact, our ancestors were stolen and sold into slavery because they were some of the best sources of hard labor in the world.

It is just a matter of having the right mindset and the right support system. You will get the mindset as a result of making up your own mind about what you will believe. The support system will come as a result of you beginning to surround yourself with many like-minded people.

## *Summary of Step 8*
## Investing to Keep Your Money Growing

Have you heard the stories about all the lottery winners who have ended up broke? Do you ever wonder how this happens; when someone is suddenly given all the money he or she could ever need to live comfortably, never needing to work again? I know the answer has to do with these people not knowing about how to make their money make money. Instead of looking for ways to keep their money growing, they spend, spend, spend, and spend, until they have spent themselves into the poorhouse. While it is true that spending money is a necessary part of making money, spending for the sake of accumulating more material things that have little or no lasting value is not going to make anyone rich. Investing is the way to make money, and my plan calls for you to invest some of your income in financially responsible and sound ways.

*Step 9*

# Share Your Wealth and Knowledge

9 What in the world does giving away time, knowledge, and money have to do with becoming a millionaire? I think most people believe it is the hoarding of these things that allow us to become millionaires. Well, there is some truth to that, but there is more to becoming a millionaire than learning how to get and keep money and things.

The millionaire mindset I am advocating is much more than that. I believe we have the responsibility to help others in need. I believe it is beneficial to everyone—the rich, middle class, and poor, to share our blessings with someone less fortunate than ourselves. There are those who are hungry, sick, or just need a helping hand. This is so important because the schools, hospitals, and the various institutions that are designed to help people never have enough money. It is our responsibility as human beings to do what we can to help out those reputable institutions. From the churches to hospitals, there are numerous social and charitable institutions and individuals that need our help.

My spiritual beliefs have led me to recognize and praise God for my blessings. Because I am grateful every day for the many things God has allowed me to enjoy in my life, I have a strong desire to help others. I believe that no matter if you are rich or poor, every time you perform some unselfish act for the purpose of helping someone else, you help yourself in the process. And since I believe it is right to use what we have earned and learned in life to help others, it is my greatest hope that as you gain financial freedom from applying the principles and guidelines of this book, that you will use your blessings to be a blessing to someone else.

I know that you and I don't hear some people who have wealth talking about how God has blessed them. I don't know why this is true, because I believe a lot of people who enjoy financial wealth believe in God. Perhaps some people separate what they have been able to accomplish in their lives from their faith in God. Maybe they feel they are personally responsible for what they have attained, and that there is no need to attribute their success to God. I believe differently.

I believe it is not only right, but it is necessary to give God the glory for what I have been able to accomplish with my life. After all, I owe my entire existence to the providence of God. Had it not been His will, I would not have been the result of the conception that occurred in my mother's womb. I take to heart these words from the Bible found in Luke 6:38, which instruct, "Give, and it shall be given unto you; good measure, pressed down, and shaken together, and running over will be put into your bosom. For with the same measure that you use it, it will be measured back to you."

## Helping Others Through Giving

Giving to help others in need is the way we demonstrate our belief in the love and teachings of Christ, every day. While it is sometimes necessary to give money in order to help someone, most often, it is best to "teach people to fish." What I mean is, neither you nor I can ever earn enough money for money to be the only thing that we give to people. Therefore, I believe it is much better to help someone learn how to earn money for him or herself. That way, instead of feeding them for one day, we can help them feed themselves for a lifetime.

Giving money to people can create dependency. If my helping someone makes that person dependent upon me, then I am not really helping. Help should be more enduring; more sustaining than some sort of temporary "financial aid." I believe God wants us to depend first and foremost on Him for all things, physical and spiritual, and I don't believe God wants you—as an able-bodied adult—to become dependent upon another human being for your monetary needs.

Interdependency is fine, because ultimately, people need other people. Therefore, interdependence is actually the ultimate way to live. But dependency, on the other hand, is not something adult human beings should want to create and perpetuate for the long term. Therefore, I believe it is much better to give to people in ways fostering financial independence. That is what giving is all about. Those who are strong should give to help those who are weaker, enabling them to become stronger.

Giving comes from strength. People who genuinely want to help others know that in order to help someone else, you must have something to give. That can mean anything from giving of your time and caring, your spiritual understanding, or your professional knowledge and skills to help those in need that don't possess the personal resources that you have.

## Time and Caring

Time is a commodity, and it is clearly valuable. None of us ever seems to have enough of it to do all the things we want to do in a day. I am a business owner, a realtor, an author, a husband, a father, a community worker, and I am involved in many different educational, professional and civic organizations and activities. I take each of my commitments to heart, because it is very important to me to do well in everything that I accept to do. Therefore, I have to understand the value of time. And since neither you nor I can inventory time, it is not something we can afford to take lightly or to spend unwisely, because once it is gone, it is gone forever.

Even with the kind of schedule I have every day, I still take time to give of myself to others. I believe doing this provides an outward demonstration of my caring for the well-being of others. It provides a living example for others. Talk is easy, but walking your talk is the real test of caring.

It doesn't matter how many times I say I care if I am not willing to do anything about it. So I make it a point to show that I care about the well-being of others. I *take time* that I could be using for myself, my business, or for some other endeavor of mine, to do good for someone else. I didn't say that I "make time," because there is no way to make any new time. I *take* time. Because that's really what any of us has to do in order to add something else to our busy lives. We have to seize the time from somewhere else; some other activity or engagement has to be moved aside or rescheduled.

Therefore, I take time away from myself, and I give it to others. I believe it is not only one of my responsibilities as a Christian to do so; it is also something that brings me joy and untold personal benefits. Although I give of my time with no expectations of reward, it is inevitably rewarding to give unselfishly. By giving of my time to others, I meet new people, reconnect with people I have not seen or heard from in a while, and learn about things I might not have learned about any other way.

It is important to me to spend some time every week or every month helping someone else in some way. The ways I give of my time may be different from ways you might think of to give of your time. I might speak to a group of people interested in finding ways to buy a home. (Since I'm a realtor, I have knowledge that can help people who don't yet understand mortgage lending or the home-buying process.) Or, I might work with a group at my church that is helping someone in need to find financing for a home or a business. But I believe it is vital to your own life and growth as a human being to take some time away from you, and to give to someone else.

## Spiritual Understanding

You don't have to be a preacher or a professional minister or evangelist to share your spiritual understanding with other people. If the Bible is your basis of understanding, I believe you have the ultimate guide for helping people help themselves through the gaining of divine wisdom for living. Use your knowledge of it to give an inspiring message to someone struggling to accomplish something positive. Use it to motivate and offer comfort or praise to people who are trying to help themselves and others. Sometimes, a positive word from someone is all it might take to change someone's day. Your positive words could actually make a difference today, in someone else's life.

## Knowledge and Skills

There are many ways you can use your knowledge and skills to help others. If you have a college degree, there is a good chance you know a lot about something. If you have a career field, whether it is what you studied in college or not, you have learned a lot that you use every day to earn a living. Knowledge and information are powerful things. They can be used to uplift and change lives. You can use what you know to help people who need, but who do not have the education resource that you already possess.

What are some ways you can give of your knowledge and skills to help those in need? Here are a few of my suggestions:

- Volunteer to be a tutor for underprivileged children.
- Set up a workshop or a seminar through your church, offering to help people—free of charge—using your knowledge and/or skills. If you're a tax expert, help people with basic tax questions. If you're a mortgage loan officer, teach low-income people about how to find help with financing a home. If you're a counselor or a college professor, offer advice or counseling to needy high school students who want to go to college.
- If you are proficient or an expert at doing something, help someone who can't afford to pay experts. For example, if you are a professional writer, help someone who has the skills to go into business to write a business plan for starting for a new business.

There are many different ways you can give of yourself to help others. If you are a leader, either in your professional career, or in your community service activities, you can model the ethics, values, and behavior you want to see in others. Doing this is the best way to continuously develop and refine your own leadership skills. Giving is a process of discovery and learning. When you give unselfishly to others, you always reap the kind of rewards that no other activity can bring.

## Don't Forget to Give to Yourself Too

As you learn to give of yourself, you should also remember to "re-fuel" by giving *to yourself*. Your personal development is vital to your being able to help other people. As you work to acquire greater financial freedom for yourself and your family, you're going to become the owner of multiple properties, and you might even be starting your own business. Either or both of these endeavors could land you in a leadership spot, where you might have several or many people working for you. Therefore, it is going to be in your best interest, and in the best interest of your dreams for increased financial security, to develop and grow your own knowledge and skills.

It is easy, when you are the leader, to believe you have "made it," and that there is nothing more you need to learn or to do. It is easy to see yourself as someone who can direct people to "do as I say, not as I do." But this attitude will not gain you respect. It will only ignite mistrust and fear, things that are opposed to respect. When you lead others through use of fear, no one grows, and there is no personal development. Therefore, if you feel you need to lead others through the use of "fear tactics," then you are in need of professional development as a leader.

You can set positive examples for others who look up to you by working to reach your own highest potential. In your organization, you should be the best example of what you want others to aspire to become. The more you work on improving yourself, the easier it will be for you to get people in your organization to work on improving themselves. Your example will make it easier for others to become involved in personal development.

With your support and involvement in personal and professional development activities and opportunities, you are showing everyone in your organization that you not only care about their development, but that you consider their career and personal growth to be a vital part of what they can offer your organization. It is much more important for you to be a "living example" of what you want others to aspire to, rather than just providing "cheerleading" as motivation. While cheerleading is very important, motivation is more genuinely accomplished from the inside out, rather than from the outside in. "Hooray, hooray" cheerleading speeches are an example of "outside-in" motivation. Offering people opportunities to improve their training, education, skills and ultimately their lives, is "inside-out" motivation. Which would motivate you more?

## Igniting a Cycle of Help

I do not believe it is possible to do a good thing for someone else, and not reap some kind of personal benefit from doing it. And while you should give of your time, knowledge, attention, loving concern, or charitable support to those in need without requiring a reward for doing so, it is still inevitable that rewards will come to you. That's just the way God seems to have set things up. As we are told in Galatians 6:7, "Be not deceived; God is not mocked: for whatsoever a man soweth, that shall he also reap." With this in mind, as leaders or as followers, we should always be mindful of what we are sowing, because ultimately, that is what will come back to each of us.

Therefore, in your quest to sow good seeds, you can use your professional or career-related expertise to support community-based volunteer organizations. Your knowledge and/or skills can be used to help sustain and expand community service, empowering people by teaching them how to do more to help themselves. .

When people help other people by giving unselfishly, we all benefit, and we all have something to give. You might be able to help someone find basic housing or emergency food. You might be able to help someone learn to read, increase/enhance their education, or find new training opportunities. You might be able to help provide activities for young people from low-income families who cannot afford to pay to keep their children active during the summer when school is out.

I believe when you help others, you actually gain a greater understanding of your own purpose in life. You begin to understand how all of us need each other, and that you need the person or people that you help just as much as they need you and your help. I believe this is true because when we are able to let go of personal gain as our reason for giving of ourselves, we actually grow as human beings.

I believe we actually learn to care for ourselves better, and to appreciate our blessings, by taking care of someone else. For example, we learn the true value of literacy by teaching someone to read. We make our community better and safer for everyone living in it, by counseling and caring about wayward teens. In addition, when we help to uplift people who are in need, we are providing them with the ability to help themselves and others.

Therefore, instead of needing gratitude, when you help someone else, ask the person you help to "pass it on." Ask them to help someone else in need whenever they are able to do so. If you ask them to, the person you help one day will surely help others. That means your act of love towards someone else can begin a circle of giving that will ultimately give back to you, as the circle of giving is completed.

We learned from the Bible, through the "Parable of the Talents," that God wants us to use what He gives us. We are to make use of what we have, and we are not to bury our potential or hide it away in fear that we'll lose it. In fact, fear of losing what we have is the surest way to bury our potential. Having the faith and courage to use what you have is what will bring abundance to you.

Throughout this book, I have been discussing with you ways to use what you have to increase your financial freedom. And although I have recommended that you begin a savings plan, I have tried to impress upon you that it is not likely that you will save your way to wealth. Most of us who work for a living just will never make enough money to be able to save enough money to create real wealth. For this reason, we have to learn how to use some of our money to plant seeds that will enable us to grow more money.

Well, just as we have to use money to make money, we also have to give what we want, so that we can get what we want. What? Yes, I said give what you want, and you'll get what you want. If you want people to respect you, give them your respect. If you want to increase your business, help someone else (in a different line of business) bring more customers to their business. You'll learn a lot about how to help yourself by helping someone else. When you're feeling down, help cheer up someone else. You'll be surprised at how fast your own mood will change for the better.

## Unselfish Giving Will Ignite Real Prosperity

I believe the best contribution you can make to the world is to help someone else to become a giver. When you feel blessed, it makes you want to give unselfishly. And when you give of yourself unselfishly, you will be rewarded. When people see you giving without expectation of gain, you ignite within their minds a light of hope for humanity.

Your rewards will come in all forms of prosperity, not just in monetary ways. The word "prosperity" refers to more than financial gain. You can be "prosperous" in ways related to:
- Health
- Personal happiness
- A good and nurturing relationship with your spouse
- Loving, caring friends
- A job or career you enjoy
- Raising loving, honest children
- Living in a community you helped to make safer

A lot of people seem to actually fear having or wanting more. And I'm not just talking about more money. It seems to me people truly "dare to dream" about having true prosperity in all aspects of life. It's as though we feel we're not worthy, or that it just cannot happen for us. The truth is, all things really are possible, if you only believe. And I believe you will be more prosperous in all aspects of your life when you learn the principle of unselfish giving.

Unfortunately, there is almost a "stigma" associated with desiring monetary abundance. After all, we don't have to look very far to find examples of people with money being ruthless, vile, mean-spirited, greedy, self-centered, and dishonest. We see them on the six o'clock news. We see them falling from grace, and going to prison. So I know why a lot of people feel that money is the cause of people exhibiting such negative character traits.

But if you believe that having money makes these people act this way, you're wrong. It is not the having of money, but the loving and gluttonous hoarding of money that brings to the surface character traits these people already have. In their zealous quest for more and more money, they neglect doing the personal development work they need to do. For too many people, it's true that "power corrupts" and that "absolute power corrupts absolutely." A lot people who have "made it" feel that no further work on their character is needed. I believe that the opposite is true. When you have money and power, you need even more work on your character so that you can do the right thing with what you have. The Bible, in I Timothy 6:10, says, "For the love of money is the root of all evil: which while some coveted after, they have erred from the faith, and pierced themselves through with many sorrows."

It's unfortunate, but once some of the lovers of money fall from grace, all it seems to take is spending some time in prison reflecting on who they have become for many of them to then begin doing the work needed to build their character. I often wonder why couldn't they see the need for the work before going to prison? I believe the answer is related to one word: Humility. Falling from grace and going to prison brings some of them to the realization that they are not "invincible." They realize that having a lot of money does not make a person "perfect," and then they are able to begin the process of learning and improving.

For a lot of other people, it is not until they become very old—when they begin to feel frail and vulnerable, that they begin looking to God for understanding and guidance. I'm doing it differently. I'm looking to God for wisdom, understanding, and guidance while I am able-bodied and strong. I am looking to God for wisdom while I can use my blessings of prosperity to help myself and other people. I'm not waiting until I am "broken" physically, to find my humility, or my need for God's strength.

God desires us to be humble in spirit because in our "brokenness" we reach out to him, relinquishing all claims to control. Once we do this, we begin the long and demanding road to spiritual growth. When we're under the belief that we have nothing to learn, no learning can take place. Once we let go of that fallacy, God is able to work with us. Just as arrogant pride blocks the entrance to learning—humility opens it up.

## *Summary of Step 9*
## Share Your Wealth

One vital part of the millionaire mindset I want you to develop says it's better to give than to receive. Most of the time, we think of giving as being the opposite of getting, but giving actually is getting because whenever you give away something of value, you're always going to get something of value in return. It may not be something that is measurable in terms of dollars and cents, but—believe it or not, the most valuable things in life are not, because they are priceless.

*Step 10*

# Plan Your Estate

10 If you follow the steps as outlined in this book, on your way to becoming a millionaire, you will accumulate an estate consisting of some or all of the following types of property:

1. Personal Property
2. Real Property
3. Business
4. Insurance
5. Benefits or income

Once you have accumulated this estate, then you must decide what you will do with it when you pass on from this world. You could do like most Americans and make no plans for your accumulated wealth. If you choose this road, however, the state in which you live will decide what to do with your assets. On the other hand, you could follow the example of smart people with foresight, and make plans to control your estate even after you are laid to rest.

None of us likes to think or talk about death, but it will surely come even if we don't think or talk about it. The time of death is predictable only in cases of suicide. Therefore, we all know death will come one day, but we don't know when. That is why we must plan to live a long life while, at the same time, we must make a contingency plan in the event our time is cut short.

You and you alone should determine how you want your estate

distributed. After all, you will have spent much of your life obtaining the education, training and skills needed to earn the money and accumulate the wealth that makes up your estate. The only way for you to have maximum impact and influence while you are in the grave is for you to make a will setting out how you want your estate distributed.

## Most Americans Do Not Have a Will

Did you know that more than 70% of Americans do not have a will? For one or more reasons, people seem to shy away from preparing them, as if not having one is going to postpone death. Not true. The lack of a will won't add even one day to your natural life span. However, not having one will add a lot of confusion to your family's life if you should die prematurely, or even if you live to a ripe old age and then die, without one. You need a will. Why? A will—which I believe is part of a "millionaire mindset," is needed to control who gets your property, who will manage the estate you have accumulated, and even who you would want to have guardianship of your children, upon your death.

If you die before drawing up a will to guide your assets, you could create a very costly process, both financially and emotionally, for your heirs to obtain possession of your assets. While you are living, you can derive some satisfaction from knowing that by planning ahead, your influence and direction will continue after you are gone. As a matter of fact, that is about the only way to ensure that what you want will be done. Also, you will live on through your will. Your ideas, your plans, and your passion for achieving your objectives will live on based on how you set up your will.

I've seen numerous cases in my real estate practice where someone has lost his spouse and cannot sell property from the estate. That's because when there is more than one "heir," an estate becomes "heir property" if no will has been left specifying exactly who is to get control of what.

## What Happens When You Die Without a Will?

People who die without a will leave all their assets for the state to distribute. It's true. You are the only person who determines whether your family or the state inherits the right to distribute your estate after you die. If you leave this decision to the state, your estate will be divided in a way that is determined by the government. If you live in a community property state, your community and joint property will pass to your spouse. Your part of your property will be distributed in this way:

1. If you have a spouse, your spouse receives all of your property if you leave no children, parents, siblings, nieces or nephews.
2. Your spouse receives half of your property if you leave one child or one or more parents, siblings, nieces or nephews.
3. If you leave two or more children, one-half of your property will go to your spouse.
4. Anything you leave that is not given to a spouse is distributed to the following persons, in this order:
   • Your children, or if your children are not living, their children
   • Your parents
   • Your brothers and sisters, or, if they are not living, their children
   • Your grandparents, or, if they are not living, their children (i.e. your uncles and aunts)
   • Children of your deceased spouse
   • Relatives of your deceased spouse
   • The State of your legal residence

Do you really want the state deciding how your property will be distributed after you die? If you answer "No" to this question, then you need to take the time now to prepare a will. While you don't have to have a lawyer to prepare a will, I would recommend that you consult one for this purpose.

## Advantages of Estate Planning

Making plans for what will happen to your estate after you're gone should be an important part of achieving your dreams of becoming a millionaire. An important part of a "millionaire mindset," having a will protects your wishes with regard to how your estate is divided and distributed.

Without a will, difficulties can arise when determining who is supposed to get what portion of the assets you have accumulated. Different states have different laws, and it cannot always be assumed that the possession of property will naturally pass to the spouse. The property could become the possession of several heirs and would require that its distribution be done through the courts.

There are numerous stories told about the widow with no cash. Whether an estate is large or small, liquidity (cash) is needed to provide flexibility during the transition period immediately after death. Readily accessible money will be needed to pay taxes and final expenses. Therefore, if liquidity is not provided, the sale of some non-liquid assets such as real estate or a business may be forced upon the estate. When you are forced to sell too quickly or at a time that is not favorable, you don't receive a fair price for your assets.

A friend of mine, who is a bank officer, was telling me that he carried a small amount of insurance. He also told me that if he knew the exact time that he would die, he would surely spend his last dime prior to his death. His comments are common to many people when they think about estate planning.

- First, he hadn't made plans to distribute his estate because he didn't think it was large enough.
- Secondly, he hoped that he would be able to spend it all before he died. That means he was thinking of the cash in his bank account as his only assets.
- Finally, what he and most people fail to realize is that by our mere existence we accumulate an estate, whether we plan it or it just happens. Someone's estate might include just the clothes on his or her back. Still, whatever we accumulate in life—all our worldly possessions—will one day be distributed either by us or by the courts.

Again, none of us knows the exact time that we are going to die. Death will come at a time that is most unacceptable or what we may call "a bad time." There is simply no good time for it. Also we will leave this world just as we arrived—without possession of material assets. Since we will not and cannot take anything with us, we should prepare what we leave behind for distribution to our loved ones.

Most estates are relatively simple, consisting of a home, personal property and any investments you have. However, no estate is too small to have a will that designates specifically how you want your assets distributed. The price paid to a lawyer or others that have the expertise to handle these matters is money well spent.

In this stage of my recommended steps to becoming a millionaire, I am not trying to make you an expert in estate planning, because I am not one. I am simply trying to show you that planning for how your estate will be distributed after you leave this earth is an important consideration, and it is part of the millionaire mindset. If you are truly developing the right mindset for becoming a millionaire, it should be part of your objectives—as you are building your estate—to make sure all your assets continue to be used, as you want them to be used, after you're gone. Estate planning is the only way to get that assurance. Therefore, you should be well aware that if you want to control the distribution of your wealth after you're gone, you need a will.

If you think estate planning is a complicated yet necessary step, then my mission has been accomplished. Hopefully, you will do what my wife and I have done; that is, find competent legal help to assist you in planning your estate. With a plan, provisions will be made for how your estate will be divided and managed after death. The price you'll pay for not planning your estate is much higher than anything you will pay for planning it.

I realize that your wishes for what happens to your estate may change over the years. That is why it is important for you to know that you can make changes to the will as times goes on. Your main objective is to save your family the cost and aggravation of having to go through unnecessary legal procedures after your death.

### _Your assets might include:_
Personal Property (cash, furniture, jewelry, etc.)
Real Property (home, apartment building, other real estate)
Insurance (all types of insurance)
Business (corporation, sole proprietorship, partnership)
Benefits (pensions, social security)

**<u>*Disbursement of your assets might include distributing them among these entities:*</u>**
Government (taxes)
Family and Friends
Charity (church, hospitals, foundations, other)

*Summary of Step 10*
## Plan to Leave a Legacy

This is the last of the numbered steps in my plan to help you become a millionaire. As I said earlier in this chapter, you could do like most Americans and make no plans for your accumulated wealth. But it is my hope that you will choose for yourself what happens to your assets once you are gone. I hope you will leave a legacy for your family that will outlive you, and into perpetuity. What more wonderful and loving goal could a person have, than to leave behind something that can empower and inspire generations yet unborn. That's what you will have the opportunity to do with your wealth. It's a big responsibility, but now that you are developing a millionaire mindset, I know you can handle it.

# Believe in a Higher Power (God)

11 Once you have started following my recommendations about how to become a millionaire as an average working man or woman, you will undoubtedly find there will be times when events in your life do not go as planned, and you begin to feel there is no good reason to continue on your quest. To cope with feelings of helplessness, I believe a person must first believe they can succeed. Therefore, in order to believe in yourself through thick and thin, you're going to need something greater than yourself to fortify your strength from the inside out.

The best source of inner-strength I have found is to be spiritually connected to God as my Higher Power. That's why I believe it is very important that religion and worship play a navigating role in life. I am not proposing that you should be Baptist, Methodist, Jewish, Catholic, Hindu, Muslim, Protestant or Catholic. It is not up to me to make that choice for you. I can tell you, however, that I am Christian, and that Christianity has proven to be the best choice of spiritual "connectivity" for me. It provides me with a positive faith in a loving God, offering the uplifting, inspiring, and motivating kind of strength I need to tap into every day. When times are good, and when times are bad, I have a wonderful and unvarying refuge in my Christian faith.

Whenever I have found matters of my life are beyond my control (and even when they are within my control), I find a need for spiritual guidance and direction. When it seems like a million things are going awry, it is simply not possible for me to have within myself all that I need to work everything out. I need to be able to take all my problems, worries, stresses, concerns, burdens, and challenges, and put them somewhere where they can be worked out for me. My faith provides that kind of refuge. In fact, my faith gives me specific instructions for doing just that. It tells me I can leave all my burdens at Jesus' feet, and that if I don't do this, I'm not trusting God to help me. Now, that does not mean I don't have any work to do. But it does mean I have to let go of all the negative forces pulling at and against me, so that my God can show me His positive, optimistic way. And when I follow His guidance, I know everything will be all right, and everything in my life will proceed according to His plan. And that has always proven to be the best plan for me.

I truly believe that in order for any of us to have a well-balanced and meaningful life, it is important that we allow spiritual development to guide us. A saying I have heard often is that we are not physical beings having a spiritual existence on earth; we are, rather, spiritual beings having a physical existence. If this is true—and I believe that it is, then it just makes good sense to spend time connecting spiritually.

The question may arise, "Can you make money without God, or if you have God in your life will you make more money?" I do not have the answer to such a complex question. I do know, however, that as human beings we have limits. Our knowledge is limited. Our time is limited. Yet our lifetime challenges are many and most often difficult. To try to handle or to try and face life's obstacles alone is unwise. I am sure that whatever you're trying to do, whatever your intentions are, if you find a way to develop your spiritual beliefs along with your material goals, you will most likely multiply your chances for success. Therefore, belief in God, I feel, is crucial for every individual.

Without positive Christian thinking and principles, I believe it is nearly impossible to pull yourself up from the bottom. Without positive guidance, too many of the downtrodden amongst us, or people at the bottom of the social rung, often find themselves spending too much time hating people, complaining, feeling inferior, and groaning about what has been done to or against them. As human beings, we are equipped with the ability to exert just so much energy, and if we use that energy in the negative, we will have no energy left for the positive. My faith teaches me to use my energy in positive ways. It teaches me to love my neighbor and my fellow human beings, and to do what I can to help figure out how we can all grow stronger in every way—from a positive point of view. It tells me that no matter what someone may or may not have done to me, that hatred and meanness is wrong. It tells me peace is right. And it tells me love is right and good.

Christianity actually teaches a lot of undeniably good lessons that can be used as guidance for any businessman or woman. It provides us with a set of positive moral and ethical principles that are unwavering, and that—if applied—will always see you through triumphantly. If you choose this path, you have to allow God to teach you how to find your victories. They may not always be what you think you want, but they will undoubtedly always be exactly what you need. Some of my favorite Bible-inspired guidance/lessons:

1. *"Come unto me, all ye that labour and are heavy laden, and I will give you rest."* (Matthew 11:28)
   Guidance/Lesson: God expects us to work for what we get, and He knows we will face challenges and trials as we work. He knows that we will sometimes forget about Him and His promises, and that we will sometimes try to handle all the burdens of our daily lives, including our business or work, by ourselves. So we will undoubtedly become "heavy laden." This is true because we simply cannot handle all that will come against us by ourselves. But if we are spiritually connected, we have a place to lay our heavy burdens, a place to find rest and lightness.

2. *"Know ye not that they which run in a race run all, but one receiveth the prize? So run that ye may obtain. And every man that striveth for the mastery is temperate in all things."* (1 Corinthians 9:24-25)
   Guidance/Lesson: This says to me that the idea of competition is positive and good. It challenges us all to do our best, and to understand that not everyone is going to end up at the same place as a result of similar efforts. But that's also good, because no matter where we end up, the joy and pride is to be found in running the race, accepting the challenge, and in doing our best.

3. *"But a certain Samaritan, as he journeyed, came where he was: and when he saw him, he had compassion on him, and went to him, and bound up his wounds, pouring in oil and wine, and set him on his own beast, and brought him to an inn, and took care of him. And on the morrow when he departed, he took out two pence, and gave them to the host, and said unto him, Take care of him; and whatsoever thou spendest more, I will repay thee."*
(Luke 10:33-36)

Guidance/Lesson: Everyone but the Good Samaritan left on the roadside the man who had been mugged by thieves. But not the Good Samaritan. He took it upon himself to be the help the wounded man needed. Jesus told us we should "go thou, and do likewise." He meant we should give to others using our resources and blessings. This is not just a nice idea; it is a business principle. Jesus wants us to honor Him by helping others. He wants us to understand that it's good to have and to show compassion for others. And that it's not good to be selfish and uncaring. Hardhearted selfishness doesn't work for good in our daily lives, or in business. It is much better to be caring and giving. You don't have to wear your heart on your sleeves, or be a "pushover" for anyone. But to have loving and genuine concern for other human beings is how we all should live. Every day.

When you are truly connected to God as your Higher Power, everything that you go through will make you stronger, and all of your strength and accomplishments are a praiseworthy testimony to His goodness. Hence, a good Bible lesson emphasizing the main point I have tried to make with this chapter is found in Jude 1:24-24, where it says, "Now to Him that is able to keep you from falling, and to present you faultless before the presence of His glory with exceeding joy, to the only wise God our Savior, be glory and majesty, dominion and power, both now and forever. Amen."

*Step 12*

# Believe in Yourself

12 Make no mistake about this: the only way you are going to achieve the financial freedom I have outlined in this book is to believe in yourself and your abilities. If you believe you can do this, you can. If you believe you cannot do this, then you cannot. It is just that simple.

There is nothing about me that makes me so patently different from you that I can become a millionaire, and you cannot. The difference might be only that I have always believed I could become a millionaire. I have always known that if I believe in my hopes and dreams and that if I work toward achieving them, that one day I would be victorious. I knew I would create wealth and financial security for my family and myself, and that I would have something of great value to leave for my grandchildren, and their grandchildren (Proverbs 13:22). I knew this because I had a great role model in my father and mother, and I have a sustaining faith in Jesus Christ that keeps me constantly supplied with the confidence to keep on believing in my God-given abilities, and that keeps me working conscientiously and passionately to achieve my dreams.

This "mini-chapter" is, therefore, devoted to reminding and encouraging you that in order to climb the steps I've outlined for greater financial freedom, you are going to need to keep up your confidence in yourself and in your ability to accomplish each step.

## Believe in Yourself Wholeheartedly

How do you begin to believe in yourself? Is it some kind of mind-over-matter trick that only a few people learn to master in life? Or is it something simpler than this that just about anyone can master? I believe it is the latter.

I believe the first thing you need to do is to make sure that you truly believe in yourself, wholeheartedly. You must believe that you are who you say you are, and that you can do what you think you can do. In other words, be true to yourself. Be ready to work on any aspects of yourself where work is needed. If there is something you need to learn before you can begin working on achieving your dreams, then get started on the learning process. If there are changes you need to make in your lifestyle so that you can begin a savings plan, make those changes. You must be willing and ready to do the things you know you'll need to do in order to get the ball rolling. If you're not willing to do what's needed, then you are not ready to do this.

## "See Yourself" Accomplishing Your Goals

One thing I do whenever I want to accomplish something is to see myself actually achieving that goal. Let me say it again. When I make up my mind that I want to do something, I see myself—in my mind's eye, accomplishing whatever it is I want to do. Because I believe if I can see myself accomplishing my goal I am halfway there towards actually accomplishing it. Anything I think I might want to do, that I cannot literally see myself doing, I know I most likely will not be able to do. Whenever you or I desire to achieve some goal, yet allow words to come to mind such as, "I cannot see that happening to me," or "I can't see myself doing that," we are—in fact—refusing to allow our mind to show us what we are capable of doing.

Just imagine that you want to take a vacation on a Caribbean cruise. You just finished watching a DVD about this cruise with all the accompanying enchantment, food, and fun. The only problem is you don't have the money you need to pay for the cruise for yourself and your spouse. The cost of the cruise vacation is $5,000, and you don't want to dip into your savings (because you're saving to make a purchase of a new real estate property).

You decide to take steps towards making this dream come true, without using your savings. After all, you deserve a vacation, and so does your hard-working spouse. You make an action plan for accomplishing this dream, with the first step being to visit a travel agency to find out how they might be able to help you discover ways to afford this vacation. Pinpoint Travel (a made-up name) tells you they can hold your reservation for as long as 90 days. That means you and your spouse now have three months to earn the money you need. So the two of you begin thinking about what you can do to earn the money. You both work full-time jobs, but have plenty of time in the evenings. You are sure that if you put your heads together, you will come up with an idea that will work.

You stop at one of your favorite fast-food restaurants on the way home from the travel agency, and your spouse notices a sign on the wall announcing that Willie's Wonderful Chicken (a made-up name) is looking for two part-time workers. You talk to the manager and discover that if both of you work there part-time for three months, together, you will clear about $6,000—and that's $1,000 more than you need to pay for your vacation. You apply for the jobs, and are hired on the spot.

It's not easy going from work every day to waiting on people in a fast-food restaurant for four and five hours, then working all day on Saturday. But you both are keeping your eyes on the prize—and that makes it a lot easier. 90 days later, you have reached—and exceeded—your goal of earning $5,000. You go back to Pinpoint Travel and pay for your vacation, and now all you have to do is give notice at Willie's (you always knew they'd be able to replace you in a flash), make arrangements with your jobs to be off for vacation, and pack!

Congratulations. You now see what it takes to accomplish any financial goal. Keep in mind that everything is first created mentally, before it is manifested physically. The Sears Tower in Chicago was first created in the mind of the developer, then the architect visualized it and drew the plans, and finally, the builder built the tower. The same process holds true when it comes to your goal of becoming a millionaire. First, you must be able to see yourself going through the necessary steps you need to go through in order to manage your life and your finances in such a way that you can become a millionaire. See yourself beginning a new habit of saving. See yourself becoming more adept at keeping a good credit rating, and doing the things you need to do to keep it good—paying bills early, not just "on time"; keeping an eagle eye on your debt and not allowing it to get out of control; and watching your spending like a hawk. See yourself finding creative, legitimate ways to earn more money when necessary, so that you don't have to miss out on doing the things you want and need to do to relax and enjoy your life. See yourself becoming a better manager of your own money, and your goal of becoming a millionaire will truly become within your reach. You must be able to see yourself in possession of your financial fortune before you will be able to acquire it.

Now. Believe that it will be just as easy to see yourself accomplishing any of the goals I have talked about in this book as being part of the millionaire mindset. Most importantly, see yourself committing to a savings program using my "cruise control" method, so you'll have the money to invest in your first property. See yourself managing your money well so that you will be able to purchase your second, then third property. See yourself starting a business that you've always dreamed of owning. See yourself being challenged, encountering obstacles, finding solutions to problems, and ultimately realizing your dreams of enjoying greater financial freedom. If you have a positive spiritual connection, you should believe that you could rise above any failures or downfalls, and that if you keep striving, you will be victorious. You will reach your goal of using the money you make as a working person to become a millionaire.

## Develop "Action Steps" for Accomplishing Your Goals

Once I can see myself accomplishing a particular goal, I develop "action steps" to keep me on track. I write them down, or I just determine the process I need to follow, and commit that to memory in small, easy-to-remember compartments. Once I finish with one part of the process, I begin on the next part. That way, I've divided what might be a "big" project into a series of smaller steps. This makes it easier to reach milestones—those small victories that will come as soon as I finish each small step.

I find that doing this helps me to hold on tightly to my determination and belief that I will accomplish my ultimate goal. Determination plays an integral part in holding onto self-confidence. Without determination and belief that I will accomplish my ultimate goal. Determination plays an integral part in holding onto self-confidence. Without determination and willpower, it is easy to allow stumbling blocks or problems to become hindrances to your success. With determination, you will develop the stamina and perseverance you will need to gain any knowledge you need, and to overcome any obstacles, so that you can proceed.

## When Negativity Comes Against You, Be Steadfast

When you encounter people—even family members and friends—who do not believe that you can accomplish your goals, your determination will sustain you in the face of any doubt and/or negativity. When people don't fully understand what you are doing, they will sometimes voice doubt, disapproval, opposition or harsh criticism. Some of them might even say that you have lost your mind, or call you crazy. But as long as you keep your faith in yourself strong, you will be able to overcome any type of negativity, no matter the source. And the good news is, as soon as you start seeing small successes, many of those "nay sayers" will change their tune. But whether they do or not, your success is going to depend on *your* belief in you, not on theirs.

You will be surprised at the number of people who will develop greater respect for you when they see you believing in yourself wholeheartedly, and working hard (and smart) to achieve your dreams. You must surround yourself with positive, supportive people, and navigate around the negative, pessimistic types. Having a strong and positive belief in yourself and your abilities steers you to toward positive people and positive experiences.

Don't be just a "fair-weather" friend to yourself. Believe in yourself through thick and thin, through good times and bad. Know that nothing worth having comes easily. You have to work for it. And every time you are tested through challenging and trying times, you are growing stronger. Gold is refined by fire. Unexpected setbacks and even failures along the way are there to test your might, and to strengthen your resolve. Expect the unexpected. Prepare for it; be ready to deal with Murphy's Law ("Anything that can go wrong, will go wrong"). Do your research to develop a foundation for understanding the business aspects of what you are doing as best you can, but learn to trust your God-guided instinct and intuition. If you develop the right mindset, and follow your plan, your steadfastness will pay off, and I know you will most certainly become a millionaire, and accomplish many of your other dreams as well.

# Develop an Action Plan, and Get Started

**13** First, I have to say there is nothing I can say here to inspire someone who is not ready to acquire more. Next, I have to say there is not much more I need to say to those who are ready to acquire more.

If you are truly ready to pursue the path I've outlined in this book, then you have already begun making a list of things you need to do to get started. You may have made this list in writing, or you may have just started making a mental list of what you are going to do next. My point is, if you are going to do this, you are already convinced of that fact by now, and there is nothing I'm going to say here that will make the difference for you. Therefore, in this brief chapter, I am simply offering additional guidance for those who are ready to do what it takes to become a millionaire.

As a working person, you already know your time is limited. You know you are going to have to make some sacrifices, change your lifestyle as needed, and prepare to do what it takes to achieve your goal.

Once you develop your own action plan, I urge you to use it to make a millionaire-to-be "to do" list every day, or at the beginning of every week. Make sure you accomplish at least something every day to move yourself closer to meeting your goals.

Your action plan will help you to take critical steps towards developing a more solid plan or path for achieving greater financial freedom. It will allow you to always know where you are now, and what things you need to do to continue putting your plans into action.

I have prepared a set of points that you can follow, or that you may use to develop your own action plan for achieving your goals.

**Action Point #1:** *Enlist the support of your spouse, children, and close family members.* Tell them what you want to do, and ask for their moral support. Ask them to help you in any way they can. For example, if you have a family member who is particularly good at Internet research, enlist their help in finding information. Give everyone a small task or area of responsibility so they'll feel they are part of your dream. Because they are.

**Action Point #2:** *Identify your goals.* Now that you've gotten your family involved, sit down with them and talk about what you ultimately want to achieve financially. Talk about what kinds of things you all want; talk about what constitutes happiness for you. Start visualizing what you are working for. Do you want a nicer home, a college fund for your children, a vacation home, the ability to travel more, to give more money to a charitable cause, or just to retire early? Decide what are some of the things you want to do as a result of becoming a millionaire, and it will be easier to begin working towards your goals. Be as specific as possible when developing your goals, because this will make it easier for you to visualize yourself doing the work you are going to have to do to make your dreams a reality.

**Action Point #3:** *Prepare yourself to take a calculated risk* (and I am not talking about gambling at the casinos). Understand that with any kind of financial investing comes risk. Be prepared for that risk. Make sure you have saved well, and that the money you use for your investment will not be missed from your every day financial obligations. If you do this, you are developing a millionaire mindset, preparing yourself for the risks that are associated with any investment.

**Action Point #4:** *Knowledge.* If you do not already have an educational foundation of some sort, I suggest that you get some basic training. Some people who want to become investors in real estate study for and get their real estate license. You don't need a license to buy real estate, nor do you need one to sell your own property. You only need a license if you want to sell real estate for other people. So you don't really need a license to become an investor in real estate, but becoming a real estate agent could give you a good understanding of everything involved in the process of purchasing and selling real estate. And obtaining a real estate license is something anyone with a high school education is qualified to do. There are all kinds of programs, many online, where you can obtain a real estate license in a few or several months.

**Action Point #5:** *Prepare yourself to work more.* Now you are going to have to put in more hours than when you were simply working for a wage. You are going to have to develop the mindset that you are going to do the work required to realize your dreams. That means you are going to have to look at your time after work (when you get home from your regular job, if you have one) as time you will have to spend with your family, and with your new endeavor. As a matter of fact, you might think of your new endeavor as a new member of your family, because it will require nurturing and cultivating in order to become a reality. So map out a few hours every evening, and devote this time to getting your business and investing plans underway.

# Conclusion

My plan to help make you rich, *The Working Man and Woman's Guide to Becoming A Millionaire*, seems so simple and so easy that some may discount its value. However, I've read in a number of publications and heard it said a number of times that it really takes only one good idea to make money. Most often, it seems to me, the ideas that make the money are indeed very simple.

For any book or any plan offering self-help advice for achieving worthwhile goals, some advice is going to be more important; it is going to carry more weight. In this book, all the steps I have outlined are important and should be understood and put to use. However, one step stands out above all the rest, and that step is Step 2, "Cruise Control."

Cruise control is about saving money. Every person that has a livable income or sustaining amounts of money coming in on a regular basis can save money. When you are young—say 35 to 40 years old, or younger, and you implement the cruise-control savings program, continuing it until you are 65 years of age or older, your success in becoming a millionaire is guaranteed.

To make sure you achieve your goal of becoming a millionaire, you have to have this money deducted from your paycheck or drafted from your bank account or credit card every month. This process puts your savings, and your dream of becoming a millionaire, on cruise control. You are actually taking the savings requirement part of the plan out of your hands. Just as the cruise control buttons in your car allow it to keep the same speed all the time, this concept of control will put the same amount of money into your savings program at the same time every month—without any further action on your part. That means, just like in the book *The Richest Man in Babylon*, you will soon be able to feel and see your purse getting fat.

Because the steps of my book and my plan are so simple, any individual from any background who is willing to apply these principles can make money and become successful, as far as success can be defined by financial achievements. Whether you want to improve your standard of living, provide for your retirement, provide protection for your family, or become a millionaire, this plan for increasing your financial freedom is recommended as a stepping-stone to your victory. By following the steps of my plan, it is impossible not to achieve your dreams. I know, because I have followed these steps, and I have achieved what some of you are looking to achieve.

Putting these steps to work at an early age is important. That does not mean an older person cannot expect to achieve financial freedom, it just means you will have less time to accomplish your goals than someone who is younger, who has the advantage of more working years left. Therefore, it is important that you should begin implementing this plan as soon as possible. The older an individual gets, his or her chances of becoming a millionaire lessen. Also, the older you are when you start this plan means more is required from you in a shorter period of time. An older person will need to put more money on cruise control each month, in order to make up for time lost in beginning the program.

The most important ingredient to achieving results from *The Working Man and Woman's Guide to Becoming A Millionaire* is getting started. This plan does not require you to be an expert. You don't need a whole lot of advanced education or knowledge to do this, and it is not a prerequisite that you make a lot of money before you start. If you've read this book, you know that everything I have suggested is within your reach. Therefore, I would bet that the biggest obstacle you are facing right now has nothing to do with a lack of education/training, or even a lack of money. I would bet that your biggest obstacle is procrastination. Most people, including me, are guilty of procrastination. However, at some point you will have to make the decision to get started and you will have to stick with your plan to completion.

Some people are procrastination addicts. They keep putting it off and putting it off until one day they wake up and 10 or 20 years have past, and then they think it is too late to go after their dreams.

Then they begin to say, "If I could roll back the clock a few years," or "If I was as young as you." They've switched from "I'm going to" and "I'm fixing to" to "If I were just." Well, one thing is for sure. None of us can turn back the hands of time. So wishing along those lines is truly a waste of time. But what you can do is rekindle the fire and enthusiasm you had in your youth, and start going after your dreams today. Why? Because what matters most is your ability to stick with it. Many times, when we begin something, we give up before we ever know if we could have been successful at it. So, your ability to stay with the plan is crucial. Someone who is 25 who begins this plan and stays with it for three years is not likely to be as successful as someone who is 45, who begins it and stays with it until they are 65.

You see it doesn't really matter what stage of life you're in. What matters is getting started, and staying with the plan. That's the key. If you are older when you begin using my plan, you will simply need to put more money on cruise control each month than you would have needed if you'd started at an earlier age.

Plan to achieve your goals. You've developed an action plan, and you and your family (if you have one) know what you want to accomplish. If you are single, you have decided what you want to accomplish for yourself. All that's left now is for you to begin working your plan. Now you need to begin targeting time frames in which to reach your specific goals, compartmentalizing your tasks by breaking them up into more manageable segments. From time to time, you might have to revise some of your plans, or rearrange a time frame. This is to be expected. But don't let things like this deter you from your plan. Make the necessary adjustments, and move on.

You might need to go back and read this book again, once more or several times, to crystallize the steps within your mind. Do that. And keep the book handy so that you can refer to it anytime you need to. If you need a pep talk, read those chapters that make you feel like you can do this, because you can. Use the book as an integral part of your process for becoming a millionaire by first achieving greater financial freedom.

That is why I wrote this book—to be your blueprint for becoming a millionaire. I have already applied every principle I am recommending to you, and they have worked for me. I am convinced they will work for you too. Good luck, and may God bless you and your efforts.

# Endnotes

Clason, George S. (1988). *Richest Man in Babylon.* New York: Signet.

Mortgage Bankers Association (May 6, 2004) National housing survey shows that key "Gaps" pose a challenge to expanding homeownership: Most Americans view homeownership as best of both worlds—a safe investment with a lot of potential. Retrieved December 2005 from www.mortgage bankers.org/industry/news/04/0506a.html

Peal, Norman Vincent (1982). The P*ower of Positive Thinking.* New York: Ballentine Books.

Wilhelm, Ian. (April 4, 2002) Foundation assets sag; nation's largest grant makers see decline of 10 percent. *Chronicle of Philanthropy.* Retrieved August 2004 from philanthropy.com/free/articles/ v14/ i12/12000701.htm

# About the Author

Al Herron is president and chief executive officer of Century 21 Galloway-Herron, in Dallas, Texas. With more than 30 years of real estate experience, he has helped thousands of working men and women realize their dream of home ownership.

After beginning his education at Alcorn State University in Lorman, Mississippi, Herron earned both a bachelor's degree and an MBA in finance from the University of Southern Mississippi in Hattiesburg. He began his career as a loan officer for Dallas Federal Savings & Loan.

After meeting prominent Dallas businessman C. A. Galloway, Herron's dreams—and his career—took a different direction. Galloway and Herron became business partners, forming Galloway-Herron Realtors, joining the Century 21 franchise in 1979.

Today Century 21 Galloway-Herron has a sales staff of more than 60 sales professionals and is consistently ranked as one of the top producing Century 21 offices in the North Texas region. The office has won the distinction of "Centurion" within the System, and was the first office to receive the coveted Century 21 Quality Service Award. First bestowed upon the company in 1992, in 2002, Galloway-Herron won the award a second time.

A well-known and widely respected member of the Dallas Business Community, for many years Al Herron has given freely of his time to organizations such as the United Way and the Dallas Fort Worth Airport Board. He is a member of the Dallas Association of Real Estate Brokers, Alpha Phi Alpha Fraternity, National Association of Real Estate Brokers, State Fair of Texas Board of Directors, and is a member of the Advisory Board of the Business School of his alma mater, the University of Southern Mississippi. Additionally, he serves on the Fannie Mae Advisory Council and the Board of Trustees for St. John Missionary Baptist Church in Dallas. In 2003, Herron was elected president of the Dallas/Ft. Worth Century 21 Broker's Council. He has been honored over the years with recognition for his work ethic and demonstrated concern for the community by organizations including the Dallas Black Chamber of Commerce, the Southern Christian Leadership Council (SCLC), and the Interdenominational Ministerial Alliance of Metropolitan Dallas. In 2002, the South Dallas Business and Professional Women's Club selected Herron to receive their "Trailblazer" award.

A familiar voice to many in Dallas, Herron currently reports on KKDA radio's "The Real Estate Report," and is the former host of "Let's Talk Real Estate" on KHVN-97 radio. He has appeared as a guest speaker at many venues around the country, including the Century 21 National Convention, The National Association of Real Estate Brokers Convention, and at conferences in Chicago, Atlanta, Las Vegas, Houston and Louisville. His first book, *Ten Steps to Financial Freedom*, was published in 1988.